The Guidance Within

The Guidance Within

Gordon Ellison

BALBOA.
PRESS
A DIVISION OF HAY HOUSE

ISBN: 978-1-4525-4978-1 (sc)
ISBN: 978-1-4525-4977-4 (e)

Balboa Press books may be ordered through booksellers or by contacting:

Balboa Press
A Division of Hay House
1663 Liberty Drive
Bloomington, IN 47403
www.balboapress.com
1-(877) 407-4847

Because of the dynamic nature of the Internet, any web addresses or links contained in this book may have changed since publication and may no longer be valid. The views expressed in this work are solely those of the author and do not necessarily reflect the views of the publisher, and the publisher hereby disclaims any responsibility for them.

The author of this book does not dispense medical advice or prescribe the use of any technique as a form of treatment for physical, emotional, or medical problems without the advice of a physician, either directly or indirectly. The intent of the author is only to offer information of a general nature to help you in your quest for emotional and spiritual well-being. In the event you use any of the information in this book for yourself, which is your constitutional right, the author and the publisher assume no responsibility for your actions.

Any people depicted in stock imagery provided by Thinkstock are models, and such images are being used for illustrative purposes only. Certain stock imagery © Thinkstock.

Printed in the United States of America

Balboa Press rev. date: 06/08/2012

Dedication

*"Linear times as we recognize are a state of physical illusion.
Our true state of being is always, forever and constant."*

This book is dedicated to those who have walked with me in this life as well as in my past. I acknowledge and thank my angels, guides, ascended masters, and teachers. I also acknowledge the Universe, Mother/Father God, and the life force; which is the source of our existence. I dedicate this book to each moment of my experience in life, as well as to those readings which I have had the pleasure to be part of.

Furthermore, this book is dedicated to all those who wish to dwell between the awake, awakened state of understandings and to those who remain to be asleep. I wish you the best in your journey and for you to come to an understanding of the proof your will never come to understand among the possibilities in other worlds and parallels. Maybe when you finally all awaken from this place of illusion and reawaken in our reality, then you will understand that you portrayed your roll well. If you choose not to believe the above, at least listen to this: Between our distant and unknown relationship, there will never be enough answers, validation or proof for whatever it is you are looking for.

I would like to make a dedication to those who attend our meditation circle. From you I have learned to understand that I have become who I am through experience.

Gordon Ellison

To my wife Lezlie, I want you to know how much I appreciate who you are and all you've done to encourage me and help me see my potential. To my children, just know that not a day goes by where you're on my mind and in my heart.

And finally to you—the reader. For whom without our shared interest, this book could not have come into to fruition. I wish you all the best and hope that you find the answers you are searching for. Please feel free to share this information with whoever is looking for similar answers. If you believe in anything, believe in yourself because that's where it all starts.

Gordon

Introduction

You're probably wondering who I am? Or specifically who am I to give YOU any insight into developing your rule of first thought let alone your own "Psychic Ability?" Allow me to introduce myself. My name is Gordon Ellison and I am a Psychic Medium from Canada; born in Toronto, now residing in Fort Erie, Ontario. I speak to those who have crossed over into a spiritual dimension, those people who have not yet "left" for whatever reason.

I have been able to do this since I was a child. As I became older I went through an awakening, where I decided to offer help regarding spiritual assistance to both sides of these worlds. I currently do psychic readings and spiritual clearings at individual homes; which I haven't done since my early adult years. Many people have a hard time believing the possibilities of being psychic and I am not here to convince you. My intention is to give pure insight to some of the answers I have come to learn, some of which may be similar to your own.

As history portrays, various types of religious groups, political leaders, and other influences—that instill doubt and fear—have scoffed at the idea of a psychic. In society, fear has been used to control the general population. I will admit that I am caught off guard, and sometimes even completely surprised, to hear about a Catholic priest that would admit to psychic awareness and other related paranormal events.

I said it before, and will say it again, I am in no way here to prove anything to anyone. This book is a reminder that skeptics and I have a common stance. This agreement is that I don't believe in them just as they don't believe in me. It's a good arrangement don't you agree? That's a good point to start on. First, know that you too can do what I can regarding psychic development or mediumship. I personally feel that our best teaching to give to others is our own personal experiences, which is what I want to share with you.

With that said, allow me to begin by telling you: we never die. This so called death in which we are taught about is nonexistent. Society has categorized it as a time for mourning. In actuality we should be glad for the person who has changed; like a caterpillar into a butterfly. Life is in a constant state of transition, where we are waiting for the opportunity. In fact, we move from one point of existence to another form—it's as simple as that. With this said allow me to continue to my stories about myself, so you can see that I am no different from you.

My upbringing had an enormous amount of ups and downs. We had a large blended family of (11) children—(7) boys and (4) girls. It is one of those sisters whom I call my biological mother. She got pregnant at the age of thirteen and gave birth at fourteen. Are you surprised? She hated to admit that I was her son and god forbid that I tell anyone. I was born in an era where the Province of Ontario would take babies away given the circumstance and age of the mother. This was the original reason why my grandmother decided to adopt me. At least that's what I thought, until I found out that she would get more Welfare money for having a baby.

This is a double-edged sword. This adoption was something that I would have preferred they not do. Although given the circumstance I may not have come to write this book or become who I am today. I would not say that I have had a blessing by being adopted back into the family. It came with it's price of abandonment, instilled at an early age which has followed me into the present I prefer not to bother with most of the family members, but this is for a good reason. Cruelty can go along way. As I have been told in the past, I have chosen my parents and the experiences that I must learn from. Who the hell thought that was a good? All joking aside, we—like many families—made the best of it.

I can guarantee there is no family on this planet like the Cosbys. Every family has drama and dynamics issues; unfortunately I wasn't spared because of my psychic tuning. I say that the same applies to each and every one of us. The trick is to understand the notion and to have faith that we will make it through this. Imagine it as a theme park ride, your thrilled yet terrified. Once its all over you choose to do it again. During my childhood, I remember the few times I contacted Albert—My Grandfather or Mishomis. For the most part, if I remember correctly, he was an alcoholic who often lived on the streets in Toronto.

I have very few pleasant memories of him. One in particular was the day he asked me what I wanted for my birthday. I was about one or two years old and I asked for an airplane. Instead he brought back a popgun with a string tied to a cork at the end. Another time I remember as a very young child was a time when I was having a nap with him. The door busted open with my brothers barging in and sweeping me away, forgetting my prized possession—a fresh bottle of Pepsi. My brothers seemed to be mad at my grandfather for something, perhaps kidnapping? Eventually, as years went by I seen less of him and finally heard that he had died at St. Margarets Hospital. Some family stories speak about how abusive he was when drunk, but they never spoke about the initial cause of his drinking. I later learned from a good source, that he too was a psychic and the cause of his drinking was an attempt to get rid of the voices and images he seen.

As I was growing up I was introduced to the voices of spirits at an early age, but I told no one. A typical thing with my brothers was for them to frighten me so I wouldn't come out of bed. This happened so much that urinating in my bed was a common thing. I would commonly hear my adopted mother tell me how stupid I was. If you haven't noticed it yet, there was physical and verbal abuse while growing up. I recollect being at the end of many blows—mostly verbal—from my mother. A common phrase I heard growing up was, "you're full of crap."

I remember this particular time that she launched her thoughts to me while we were driving, while my daughter Charlene (who we call Charli) was sitting in the back seat to listening to all of this. I am also drawn to memories when my sister Marg (she prefers Maggie), would often step in. My mother tried to clip my ear with the steel end of the belt—I still have the mark too prove it—and Marg stepped in. But I am here and that is all that matters right? To this day, I still say that neither my biological mother nor adopted mother really ever cared for me. I am telling you these stories to give a brief insight into my life. As well as to let you know that there is nothing really that special about me; I am much the same as you.

As I mentioned earlier, I was introduced to the notion of spirits at an early age. I remember vividly, this one particular time how I had contact from spirit for myself. While walking home on Kingston Road in Toronto, I heard a male voice. All of a sudden I was having a conversation with him—at the age of six years old. It was normal for me to be walking around Toronto by myself; we didn't worry much like today. I remember listening to him, while he did most of the talking and then I asked a very odd question: Why am I here? The man replied directly and loudly "to learn lots." That was it—the meaning of my life. To this day I carry that message, reminding others along the way.

After this encounter, years went on and I seen numerous spirits; sometimes I listened others I ignored them. To me this seemed normal. There were times I couldn't get rid of whoever or whatever was trying to get my attention. Every year on my birthday, I had a gentleman visit me. Each time he visited he would remind me that my life would end when I reached twenty-six; there will be more about this later on.

Most of my life may have been difficult and unfair but whose isn't? I have decided not to dwell on it and instead to make an effort to better my life. I am just another human being and am no different than other psychics. I am down-to-Earth, hate lying and try my hardest to not repeat my mistakes.

Some say that they are precognitive, but I don't really believe in it. Its not that it can't happen or others are not precognitive, it's just my personal opinion. I believe that in any moment you can choose to change your perception towards the understanding of this reality as an illusion. It all depends on what you want to experience or where you would like to be in your life. To remind you of what I have said, it will be repeated often.

My intention of writing this book is to give you the basic tools to develop your intuition or to proceed from the awake to the awakening stage. Another intention is to expose the new age era by avoiding the stereotypes of fairies, unicorns and mysticism. I don't mean to burst the bubble but—I have no special powers. In fact I don't think anyone does, except for those women who are life givers during pregnancy; which may be seen as a power or gift.

Honestly, I feel that there is no room to develop your EGO. Psychics are here in attempts to help others who are not awake or able to understand the communication that is going on around them. I tried to find a book that explains the steps in developing your psychic talents. A book that is able to assist you in going from the asleep stage in your life to the awakening stage. Along my own path of self-discovery into my psychic talents, I searched for many related books. I found an array of books related to some experience in the field and stumbled upon others which were based on the author's own ego. My reason to find said book was to see if I was nuts or making things up in my head. Since then, I have come to the conclusion that I am not crazy.

At some point in your life, you may have heard through conversation or various media about entities called spirit guides or angels. I will be completely honest with you in saying that you and everyone else on this planet have some sort of guides, angels or ascended masters (or teachers, as you may know them). These "beings" are assigned to each of us prior to our existence. We meet them and have a contractual agreement, but throughout the birthing process we often forget. It's as if you are rebooted just like your computer, where in some cases it takes a while to wake up.

Everyone has guides and angels that are around them. They are here to lend assistance or help in some way, for whatever the purpose may be at a particular time in someone's lives.

Furthermore—this may be argued—your guides are NOT your loved ones or friends. This, to much understanding, is a conflict of interest. Imagine your sibling, friend or parent being assigned as your guide. Their influence may be imposed on your learning and experience, for this reason they are not your guides. Now this doesn't mean they can't come around, be helpful or visit. This just means that this is not the major roll they play; besides they have their own agenda to work on. However with this said, your loved ones can be a guide to a complete stranger. Just remember the conflict of interest thing and it may help you understand this better.

Now on the other hand, your soul mate rarely ever comes into this existence with you because your soul mate is YOU. Your soul mate is the other part of you and for the purpose of learning and understanding they cannot exist. I would like to point out that 99% of the time your significant other is not your soul mate, because your soul mate is back on the other side. Everything happens for a reason and nothing is a coincidence. The love in which we experience can exist on all different levels. Those who we have relations with and come in contact with, allow us to experience these different forms of love. In order to truly experience this you must return to the source of all creation, where your soul mate remains. This doesn't mean that we cannot connect with our significant others; it is just not the purest form of love that we understand.

On many occasions, I have had people ask me if their loved one is happy or if they are okay? I think to myself how could they not be? I mean it's heaven right? With that said I want you to know that if you do choose—not everyone does—you can act as a spirit guide to someone else. If you do choose to act as a spirit guide Samuel and Sacreah (my angels) express it as "waking up." You see, in the spirit world there is no concept of time; their time is constant. The past, present, and future exist simultaneously. Just to make a comparison, our concept of time is measured in a linear fashion—day by day, moment by moment.

The process Samuel and Sacreah refer to as waking up can start to be explained by understanding that we reside in an "illusion" or "dream state." This can be simplified as the same sensation you get when you put your head under water. When it comes time for the individual and their essence to separate, we wake up in the reality of our truest existence. Thus one could state that our perception of reality is actually an illusion. The place where were exist is known as Heaven or whatever your like to refer to it as.

Since I keep speaking about my spirit guides, I would like to take a moment and speak about them just briefly. I hadn't spoken to Samuel or Sacreah until a later age in my life. Prior to this time there had been a number of spirit guides. There was Youngam a short muscular man from Africa, and Rista a lady from Europe. There had also been Chin the Asian and Jo-en who can be described as a young hippie with long brown hair and a thin build. Guides interchange but not often. Remember that being your guide is also a learning experience for them. You are a teacher by the actions you do in your life, the results of the experience is all up to you. What you do not learn, you are bound to repeat much like the lessons from our understanding of history. Without further adieu, let us begin our journey together; this may be a new discovery for you.

As the late Bruce Lee said: Empty your cup in order for the cup to become empty. Okay, it wasn't an exact quote but the point is there nonetheless. Enjoy and share the book with whomever you like. May you become aware of your guides along this journey; if you have not already done so already. As Samuel always says, "Remember the rule of first thought."

CHAPTER 1

Hello, My Name is Samuel

I exist to bring enlightenment, to guide and inspire wherever and whenever I can. I assist with misguided information and help to direct Gordon by giving validation in his psychic readings. I am one of the guides that Gordon has and have been with him for many of his lives. I am not the type of guide, as you would commonly understand it. My presence is just as important as my actions when helping Gordon.

I am an angel assigned to Gordon. I reside on the sixth level of the order, and Sacreah—who you will also come to know—resides on the seventh level. Understand that there is no more or less importance associated with these levels, as we all have a role to fulfill. My name is seen and spelled in many ways, but is pronounced Cham'eual (sh' sound to the ch). We as angels speak through "thought" which is the most common way of communication aside from your physical world communication. Though we have made our presence known in many ways, we can also speak aloud if and when the need calls for it. There are 2 reasons for this introduction: The first is to explain who we are. We are constantly mentioned in the book and are basically those whom Gordon will be referring to. The second reason is tell you that we do exist and have for many lifetimes.

Always remember that your world and experience never truly end. A point of reference would be a caterpillar. It transforms from one stage of existence, leaving behind its vessel and then transfers into another. The same thing happens when you go through your transformation, or what is commonly known as death. If you understand this, you understand your subconscious will; nothing ends in creation. Your life cycle is one of many that will become again and again and again. At this moment you may find the idea difficult due to many reasons such as family influences, values or other inputs into a belief or disbelief. Proof is an accomplice of fear and doubt ruled by others to create confusion or disbelief.

Many of you require what you refer to as "hard proof" of our existence. I'm sorry to say that you will be disappointed, because we have nothing to prove. Nor would we radically indulge in the idea of this. Nonetheless we are here, whether or not you believe. Understand this: We are here to help, no matter what the circumstance. Through the ways of communication, you proceed to gain experience along your path of learning.

Sacreah had come to Gordon at a point of illness. At that time, he never gave too much thought about her until later on in his life. She had shown up at a friend's home and stopped some negative spirits from entering into the home he was visiting. This was a point in his life where he was more in-depth and was awaked to his psychic work. This was the moment Gordon decided that we would be in more of the forefront work. We would be beside him, assisting whenever and wherever we can especially with his psychic readings. If you ever chose to have a reading, we would like for you to know that it is we—the angels and guides. We are the ones to help keep things running steady.

CHAPTER 2

The Rule of First Thought

Given the title of this first chapter, I don't want you to get caught up in the words. The title itself "The Rule of First Thought," could even be referred to as guidelines. The following passages will be guidelines to assist you in developing self-spiritual awareness.

It's meaning is to allow you to let go of the material objects that surround our daily lives. By letting go, you take your first step into another dimension. This is not so much in the physical world but within the physicality of your thoughts. I think that it is important to understand where we are going in order to focus our thoughts to this realization. This realization of something that has always been and will always will be with you, whether you realize it or not. I think that it's best that we start with the beginning: close your eyes and leave your mind blank. How did you find that? Was it easy? Did you actually try it?

If you did try it, did you find this hard to do for a few moments? Did your thoughts come pouring in? Well listen, no one can blank his or her mind—unless you're either dead or lobotomized. Nevertheless, I used to try and figure this out whenever told to clear my mind. I thought there was something wrong with me when I couldn't do it. Your search and intent to do such will help you to achieve your personal spiritual and psychic development.

The rule of first thought, isn't hard to get used to if you just learn a few simple steps. The first thing to remember is that "first thought" always comes from those in the spirit world—your guides, angels and family who have passed on. This action happens so fast and has no effort associated. For example, have you ever had a great idea just pop into your thought? Well, that is sort of what it's like. Each person is an individual, yet they are a part of a whole—they are in the making of the cosmos. In society we are taught to be different, separate from all others and eventually we learn how to do this so well that we separate. This is why people of First Nations decent refer to everything in our life as our relations. We are all related.

Thought without effort has powerful effect. Sometimes it can bring tears to your eyes or make you literally jump for joy when you finally get that moment. What we have to do is gain the ability to differentiate between the rule of first thought and the rule of second thought. Remember what I said earlier; just think these as guidelines and not rules. This is how my angels, Samuel and Sacreah, taught me.

When first thought comes to mind, we naturally reject it. Our bodies have a built in default system that is taught, through society and other factors, to refuse such thought. The system is stimulated and forces us to process what has popped into thought. After all is processed we left with outcomes, how to react to said outcomes, and what to do next. This may seem to be a common human reaction, but I tell you it is not. What I mean is that it's not an instinct. Survival is conditioned within our DNA, essentially instinctive. The rest is influenced by the outside world and experiences. It is at this moment, where you may learn to discover "the rule of second thought." It is completely your doing with rationalized pros and cons along with a possible outcome.

To better understand the rule of first thought, you need to understand that this takes no effort and is often hard to get used to. But as I said, when you don't try and you just allow the information to flow that is when the magic will happen. Try this: ask yourself a question; you can use the second rule of thought here and think of one. Once you have the question ask it out loud and allow the answer to come. No matter what it is, don't try to make sense of it. Now I don't mean ask aloud if you should do something stupid because that's a double application of the second rule and you already know the outcome that will soon follow.

From my experience, I have learned that sometimes the information will not make sense at first. This will happen until you begin to develop your own way of listening to the messages. Through meditative practice, where you sit quietly reflect on the question, you can begin to develop and answer from within yourself.

I will let you in on a secret: there are many ways to receive messages from your guides or angels. One way would be to practice automatic writing. This is simply done by finding a quite place free from distractions. Then mentally ask for your guides to help you with the question or decision. Once you close your eyes, allow your hand to move over the paper and you will be surprised with the message that formulates in front of you. Spiritual development will take practice and lots of it. This involves a lot of things that at first may seem overwhelming. But trust me, it is worth the time and effort that is involved. How much time will it take? Well, essentially your whole life; your life will be changing and so will everything else. From the people you meet, walk by or even sit near—you will learn to pick up on emotions. This maybe even be a spirit who is standing there beside them.

You will have to learn how to share this information with a perfect stranger. In addition to this you will have to learn rejection, because often times we are told off if they don't believe in your developing abilities. Try to understand that, when the information comes to you, you will make mistakes and it is okay. How else can you gauge your successions and developments if you were constantly right all of the time?

There are a few mantras that have helped me along the way, in which I had to apply in my life path. The first was, "Do not get caught up in comparison." What I mean by this is don't try to be like anyone else, be you. There is enough room for your psychic abilities to flourish without emulate someone else. Admire them and the work they do, but be able to recognize when you are becoming infatuated and stop it. Just like any bad habit, it will be one that you have to correct from time to time. I will tell you that at first this was hard for me. Now, unless you've had your head buried in the caves of the Mongolian mountain media psychics are a big hit. Some of the well-known ones include James Van Praagh, Tony Stockwell, and Sylvia Brown; these are just a few who went through the life learning curve of psychic talents. I admire their work, but I don't get caught up in things by trying to emulate them.

In this moment of time, understand that society considers us to be individual persons. When in actuality, that's not true. We are not as individual as you like to think. We were never meant to be singular because we are all part of one "life energy source of creation." We are constantly connected to each other through vibrations.

There are people who find that they are already experiencing psychic abilities? Let's assume you are just starting out, a beginner, and are looking for more information. At some point, you will want to research and study different psychics or psychic abilities. I would say to start with meditation. Some may take an interest in learning the healing art of "Laying of Hands"—such as reiki massage. Other ways may be learning to use the tarot cards or numerology. With any path you choose, try to remember the rule of first thought.

Just remember to ignore any doubts, fears, and personal judgment you may have of yourself. One may ask: how? Well whenever you have these emotions, ask yourself why it is you feel this way. Often times, it is due to fear of failure or rejection. If you're expecting to become some sort of guru, then forget the whole idea of trying to develop anything. This notion will only enhance your ego; if you are already a guru, then you don't need any practice.

The best way to understand the rule of first thought is to remember that the thought is sudden, automatic and received with no effort on your part. Remembering to practice meditating and differentiating between your own thought, want, or desire. Once this is accomplished, you will then begin recognize when the two become intermingled and confusing. What I have been taught by my angels and guides was and still is a constant learning experience.

You may have wondered: Why hasn't he mastered this? I will tell you that life changes and so does your way of thinking. We are human and have been taught to accept so many things in involving understanding, thinking and life. Remember to use this rule and you will be able to understand if it is your thought or intention or if it is coming from Spirit. From my experiences, I have learned where and how to differentiate and apply the rule of first thought.

After understanding our disassociation towards this type of communication, we just have to just relearn how and when to use it. Following these few simple guidelines you, and anyone else for that matter, can come to truly understand the first rule of thought. This also goes hand in hand with the second rule of thought; which I will explain a little later.

These two principles are almost mirror images of each other as they are of the same importance. When you understand the two, you will notice that one will be part of the other; much like the Yin and Yang in Chinese philosophies. These are basically the opposite of each other, black versus white, dark versus light, and so on. What I mean by this is that you will have a ton of information come into your thought and the trick is to understand if this is your information or not. Is it your own ideas, thoughts, judgments or is it so fast in delivery that the information is recognized as first thought from the spirit world?

The famous singer Gene Simmons once said, "Inspiration is nonsense." If you work hard enough, you will be rewarded. I personally think that it's the inspiration that creates the drive, which initially comes from the influence of spirit as manifested by first thought. Otherwise, how else do these movie ideas about angels and heaven pop into your head? A prefect example would be the Robin Williams movie, "What Dreams May Come."

Remember the rule of first thought is a message from your guides. It comes into your thought without effort. You attempting to make sense out of the message is known as the as the rule of second thought.

CHAPTER 3

The Rule of Second Thought

This chapter will attempt to explain why we do what we do, instead of accepting what has come to us effortlessly with love. In its delivery, you may find answers to questions alongside messages of warning, encouragement, strengths and compassion. From our personal experiences in life with, we learn a habit—which becomes almost impossible to break. That habit is one that I will refer to in this book as rule of second thought. In the beginning this was a great agitator to me. When I was learning about how to discern the difference between first thought and second thought.

I will tell you that it took practice to reject such because it is as if the second thought is built inside us as an automatic response. We judge, contemplate, and often make the opposite choice of the information. On the contrary, this is a natural response from your own freewill. What I am trying to refer to is when the information comes without provocation.

This reply happens so fast that, we often have little time to think of an answer that's already present. Now this doesn't mean you should do something malicious and say that spirit said it's okay. As this is definitely your second thought.

So just how do we discern from the two without becoming confused and wondering if it is our own? Well let me first say that to understand, practice and apply takes time, trial and effort on your part. You may not get it right away. But like I said with practice, you soon will be able to tell the difference between your own want of an outcome and those which come from helpers on the other side. When I had asked this very question, Samuel had said to me: "Try to remember this which should help; that which comes in first thought is truly coming from Spirit. The second is your own doing which you try to shrug away and discern."

This is the action of the second thought. Again, this is a normal thing which is so common that humans think it is innate or has become an unbreakable habit, which neither is the case. To give you an example how this happens, use this: You are driving and have a thought to turn and take a different direction. You then think about the time it will take, thinking maybe there is a quicker way to your destination. Then by not listening to the first thought you end up stuck in traffic or are in an accident. The first thought was trying to warn you and you then find yourself asking, why didn't I just listen to myself? This is a common occurrence and yet we seen more and more people trying to pay attention to the first thought. However there are just as many, if not more, which are ignoring this and living by the second rule all their lives.

Samuel has referred to the term "contractual agreement." This is the ability to have him in my life as well as the ability to communicate with other guides of whom I work with. For the most part, Samuel and Sacreah are the ones I work with the most. Not only do I communicate with them, but I also can hear them and have seen them in the past. I have seen and spoken to Sacreah along with a few other guides. Samuel, who I met during one of my meditations, came to me as my real estate agent. He quickly changed, smiled, placed his hand on my shoulder and said, "Hello . . . I am Samuel your Guide." When I asked Samuel why he came to me that way he stated, "In order for the introduction to be accepted, your mind had to conceive the idea of acceptance." Once he completed this sentence he changed to who he truly is.

Samuel doesn't believe that it is important for him to reveal himself. He explains it this way to me: "What difference would it make, if you already know I am with you?" I don't know how else to explain this to you except to tell you that I truly know he is there. The information that is received on both ends of our worldly comprehensions is another good indication.

By now, I'm sure you are yearning to ask me a question: Do I have guides or angels? Yes, at this very moment, everyone does. I will also tell you that even those who don't seem worthy in society have guides, who may try to assist them in developing their own spiritual awareness or understanding. It's just the way this place is meant to be. When in the general public, I try not to speak aloud when speaking with my guides or other spirits; unless I'm doing a reading, workshop or lectures.

I think it is important to listen to spirit and just as equally important to listen to what your body is trying to tell you. Some examples are easy to recognize such as a reaction to something you've eaten or by how you're feeling at this very moment. Many times people ignore the obvious, which could be easily illuminated if they just listened to their body in the first place.

It can be frustrating when people come for a reading, ignore all that is said only to leave mumbling under their breath and call the following week for another reading. I try to avoid this because it is too easy to create a dependency. This also creates an opportunity for those so-called practicing psychics, who would welcome the opportunity and take advantage of the situation; by asking for spiritual guidance that would validate and help them to move forward in their lives. Like I said, everyone is psychic just some more than others. Just be careful of these types of people. Try not to judge them and understand that they are developing their own spiritual understanding. It is unfortunate that they make it harder to trust those that are truly doing the work.

The idea of second thought is complex and can get confusing at times. The general rule is don't think about it let it come effortlessly. I am not saying, don't ever ponder on a decision that you need to make. What I mean is, when applying the work with spirit just take the rule into consideration and apply where applicable. Learn to differentiate between the two and you will come to understand that the communication received truly comes from what I will refer to as the source; just because I think it sounds cool.

The source is essentially the spirit realm. I, amongst many of the angels I speak to, refer to it as home. Samuel lets me in on some thoughts and one of them is that this so called reality is actually an illusion. According to Samuel, we travel in our sleep and at the time of rebirth—back into spirit—we reach what we call heaven. Heaven is our true reality. Samuel states that while are awake, we're actually asleep on the other side; physically living out our dreams.

One of the many reminders throughout this book is for you to remain nonjudgmental towards other people. The reason for this is because, if you choose, you will be dealing with everyone from all walks of life and various backgrounds and beliefs. Choosing to remain within the confine of negative judgment is always a bad choice. This is especially true when it will likely influence the second thought and allow you to be continuously confused and misguided with the first thought.

A great benefit about developing psychically is the fact that you will get lessons from your guides on how to deal with these types of people and situations. This will happen sooner or later if it hasn't already. To those of you who are deciding to do work with your abilities, some lessons may be sooner than later. The best thing that I can say about these life lessons is that you will grow from everything you were taught, and will continue to learn with a positive end result. I am not saying never judge someone. There are jerks out there and many of them will hurt your feelings or call you down. The only thing that can be remembered is that actions of others can sometimes become your greatest teacher. Sometimes you need to grow some thick skin and shy away from being thick headed. There is a difference.

I had previously mentioned the term comparison. This essentially means don't get caught up with comparing yourself to someone else, whether they are musicians, poets or even another psychic. Admire them if you choose but the idea of getting caught up in comparison is easily done. This can lead to stumping your growth and goals. Admire those people while understanding that you are in the human understanding and it's form. Know that you will be independent in your drive towards your dreams and goals.

Many people get caught up in wanting to be like this person or that person that they become so focused on this individual. It is almost stalker like. All along they have been missing the perfect opportunity to grow and learn on their own merits. Have patience for this, as the development of your psychic ability may take longer depending on your practice and your intentions. I am also guilty, from time to time, and I catch myself comparing myself to other well-known psychics. Just be sure to do an ego check from time to time. Make sure your head is not too swollen, by reminding yourself why you're deciding to do psychic work. Maybe you're doing this development for your own purpose? Even if you are, the theory about your ego still stands.

Up until this point, I have provided thoughts on being judgmental, comparative and the rules of thought. Now go out into the world and apply this everyday in your life; this will come by practice. If you keep a diary with these events, you can refer to them as validation for the purposes of your self-esteem. Remember: Self-esteem is good and ego is bad.

Here is some food for thought from Sacreah, my guide:

Understand that the nature of your education and influences of society is often separate from your own personal experience. It's not you who we are suggesting to change nor is it your values. However, it is the way in which you are programmed to think. We would like for you to reprogram your taught on how society and others in their belief systems inject their right and might. This is only to persuade your belief to fit their schedules and ideas, ultimately feeding their own objective. Use your freewill that was bestowed unto you for learning, growth and spiritual development. Any other thought is irrelevant in attaining spiritual awareness through control.

Don't get caught up in the idealism of owning control. Once you try to control something the outcome is always the same—you loose control. It's like sand that is clenched in your fist, where sooner or later your fist will be empty. Be the opposite and allow for the opportunity to happen. You can be an influence, as can anyone else, with all that you have already done.

CHAPTER 4

Learning Lots

Now you're probably asking yourself: What does this mean? The answer that follows is regarding a question I asked when I was six years old. I was walking home one night, when I passed a store owned by my friend's parents. I remember asking: Why am I here? The fact that a six year old boy would pull that question out of thin air is mind boggling. Immediately after asking that question, I heard a man's voice respond, "to learn lots." When I turned around to see who it was, there was no one there; I distinctly remember how I felt at this time. Somehow, at my age, I totally understood what was said because it seemed so obvious to me.

Still, to this day, I ponder that same question and answer. I have just mentioned this as a reminder not to myself but to anyone else who may be asking a similar question. Whenever I get the chance, I have an uncontrollable urge to tell people the answer. I tell them that they were born here into the physical existence on their own pretense. Also that they have to understand the agreement they have—to learn lots. Each person has his or her own experience as a teaching to understand individuality.

Learning lots is not just about mental capacity it is also spiritual capacity. We are able to grow because of the accomplishments we achieve through life lessons and spiritual development. Understand that there is a thing called a "do over." An individual will be able to re-do failed tasks of this life in that of another life, until such is complete; this includes things you didn't learn or complete. This is done in order to help you grow spiritually. You will repeat time and time again, until finished and only then you move on in another time and place of being. There are those who have completed all their tasks but this is never possible as new endeavors are always coming up. In this life, complete all that you can. Along the way you may be one of many helpers, sometimes unknown. Believe it or not, you're placed here to accomplish many things by being helpers. Did you ever wonder why that stranger did that random act of kindness? You may hear someone say, "thank God you're here, I couldn't have done that without you." My point is that you, just like I, are here for a reason. There is a higher purpose for all things in the universe. Our role here, in the physical, is a very small one. In previous lifetimes we have had to collect bits of information that we have learned, in order to help us grow spiritually.

Even though we are all related and come from the same source, I often find myself wondering why we need to be separate from that source to gain the identity of individuality. Samuel reminds me this: You are all here together, from the source of creation. In unity you are all related, equal and never apart from one another. Even your most hated enemy experiences this. In your humanism, you search for your own identity of individualism. This is done in order to learn, absorb and experience—ultimately learning lots. The process of learning is not meant to hurt another person. Rather, through your curiosities you are to experiment and acquire experiences. The goal is to expand your soul and spirituality. In the end, you should have a collective essence; your true nature of existence to a continuance of life. This process is a continuing journey in your life as it will be in many others. Yes, another life—you do have more than this one. This is contrary to belief of skeptics and those alike.

When I think about the process of learning lots, it could differ in your thoughts of learning lots. Therefore, one has to define what it means in the sense of the term "a lot." You're not limited to the amount you can learn, but as the saying goes: keep it simple. People are creatures of habit and circumstance, which will make them act in such a way to accomplish what they want; even if is at someone else's expense. But as long as you keep yourself in check, you should have no worries. It's always a good idea to make sure that your intention is originally what you wanted from the beginning. This way those around you will benefit, as will you.

The key to understanding the concept of learning is to keep yourself in check. Personally, I am always reminding myself to keep myself in check and to make sure my ego doesn't get in the way of my work. If it gets in the way of my work, my self-esteem, confidence and my ever-constant learning will see the effects. When you do discover something you just learned, stop for a brief moment and try to recognize where this all fits in the moment. Thin about those involved and how it came to be. Learn to trust your instincts, gut feeling or intuition. Trust in yourself, as it is by far the most important thing you can do while learning. I would also like to mention that learning lots isn't just about learning in the most positive way. Once you come to understand you, then you can help others in a much better outcome.

Learning lots consists of taking your experiences in life and applying that experience to the moment. Think about it. What have you done to bring yourself here, at this time in your life? What experiences have opened up opportunities for you? You are in charge of your life and what is to happen to it. Many people choose to go with the flow of things and never dare to challenge themselves to venture outside their own world. Many people, think about taking the step out of the norm, but would find themselves with chills just thinking about it; let alone worry that they will no longer be part of the collective society. As you read this, you are accepting the dare to step outside of the norm; kudos to you.

On this path, you will often find yourself in many situations to do exactly as the two words mean—learn lots. Some things you will encounter will be dealing with skeptics, co-workers, family and friends. You would think that friends and family wouldn't turn away from you or make you feel stupid about your interest. But as I said, you will learn lots. At some point, you will either, (A) give up out of fear of ridicule or (B) learn to grow thick skin, keep strong and move forward with your discovery. I will tell you that like attracts like and you will attract those who will support you rather then be negative. Often times cruelty is best served to help you deal with the others whom you may come into contact with.

Personally, I think that if you can deal with your immediate family treating you this way then you have nothing to worry about. It stings the most when your mother or even your kids are negative. If you can get over that and continue to move forward then you really can accomplish anything. Besides, the best experience is your personal experience, it's just how you decide to view the outcomes. Remember the old saying, "whatever doesn't kill you, will make you stronger."

CHAPTER 5

No Room for Ego

As I have mentioned, the ego is an element that always seems to reveal itself, whether it be in general public or in a private setting. The World English Dictionary defines ego as an image of oneself, the conscious mind. Ego is based on perception of the environment from birth onwards that is responsible for modifying the antisocial instincts and modified by the conscience.

My intention at this moment is to speak about the part of our body that is hard-wired into our general make-up as a human being. This chapter is going to be about the ego and how we need to avoid its interference in the psychic world. I also want to mention confidence, which are two separate and distinct levels. I don't want anyone to confuse the two as being the same. Confidence is learned through validation and experience.

With this experience you develop confidence which is a good thing because it keeps the intention of what your doing in check. At first, keeping the ego away will be easy because its like meditating, the more you practice the better and easier it becomes. I would also like for you to recognize when ego does appears and how to deal with it. If your intention is to do psychic readings, and all you are thinking about is how you can get money and how magnificent you are—then these are your indicators. This is an obvious sign that your ego is getting the better of you. Always be honest, with yourself and others. There will be sometimes when you wont be able to do a reading for someone and if that's the case then tell him or her. By being honest they will respect you and be more likely to return at another time. They will appreciate it if you tell them in the beginning rather than at the end, to avoid wasting both of your time.

Throughout our lives we are taught many habits such as how to judge people and put others down. Even though we are unaware of what they are going through in their lives, such as anger or hatred. You see no one can actually make you angry, this is something you choose to accept. Getting upset may be a separate element that ties into this emotion. Everything that makes us who we are is tied into each other for some reason of learning. Remember that you are only human and life will often get in the way. As I have asked you earlier: Why do you want to develop your psychic abilities? Is it for you to help others where you can? Or is it to be rich and famous?

I am not saying that this isn't a good thing, because who doesn't want to be rich; perhaps only a Buddhist Monks. But if your need is to glorify yourself by showing everyone how powerful and great you are, then I say good luck; because it won't last long. Ego and self-esteem, much like confidence, is also not the same thing. They each serve a separate purpose. Self-esteem is the building block towards your confidence in yourself, which also leads to trusting where the information is coming from.

When you find that ego is making it's way in your intention, simply remind yourself why you are here and what you intended to do in the first place. Try not to be so hard on yourself, as you will have to learn to disassociate from this as much as you can. From time to time, just do a check and change your attitude accordingly. By doing this you will be awarded by those in spirit.

I want to share a true story with you, which has a lesson accompanying it. This story is not about my own ego but still is a classic example that was taught to me by another psychic. Lets just say he has a really big ego. I know that I told you not to be judgmental, but understand that I am not judging this person. I am acknowledging the result and outcome of their action. This experience had happened when I attended a psychic fair in Toronto, Ontario. I had gone with a very well known channeller and good friend, Cliff Preston; he channels the ECHO. While at this exhibition, I met some wonderful and not so wonderful psychics. Some dealt with angels, others worked with animals, and some read cards. We had been invited to a lecture, which we started to head over to. <u>Note</u>: As a requirement all the psychics involved with the fair are expected to perform some sort of mandatory speaking engagement.

When the program started, the crowd was listening intently. This person was introduced followed by applause; I often wonder if they really meant to clap or if they felt obligated. Once everything settled down, she introduced herself followed by a pleasant smile. What happened next had my mouth drop a little. The following words cam from her lips: "I would like to clear something up, once and for all! Not everyone is psychic. There are only a few chosen to do such work and have this gift". Talk about having to bite my tongue, what arrogance. The next voice in my head was Samuel, telling me to take a positive understanding from this; it's a lesson to learn from.

Each person is on their journey in life and must do what it is to help them learn lots. I wanted to send her on a journey, I wanted to rip her a few chosen words to straighten out her ego, but there it is = anger. I allowed myself to get angry towards someone, who chose to devalue others due to her "special gifts and superhuman powers." The lesson as I said was about what she did, a teaching for me directly delivered and understood. I can tell you that there will be things like this that happen to you. It is how you choose to learn, grow and use it to your best advantage. Ultimately, knowing how to recognize your ego and deal with it. When she said that, I turned to the mother and daughter in the back of the room, walked over to them and sat down. I then proceeded to do a reading and let them know that they and anyone else can do this sort of work. I told them that this gift wasn't bestowed to only a chosen few. Did I have anything to prove by doing this? No. But I did want to take away the negative impact and change the energy in that room.

These people drove 7 hours to come to me for a reading a few weeks later. I told them that there are other psychics a lot closer to them, but their reason for travelling so far was because of how I made them feel that day for a charge of $0. I will often do this when spirit warrants it. My thought on this is if those in spirit need to get a message a person when I am there, why not? Sometimes you will see or experience those travelling with their egos, but how you choose to deal with it is up to you. It is from my experience, that I refuse to do readings at any type of psychic fairs.

I had attended another psychic fair with that of my wife and friends from the meditation circle that happens at my house. This trip was an attempt to show people the atmosphere of psychic fairs as well as to just get away from the regular schedule. This fair was also in Toronto by the International Airport. Upon arriving at our destination, many had made various purchases. These consisted of aura readings, aura pictures and wikis. A wiki as defined by Wikipedia is the energy used in many forms of spiritual practice. This is a luminous radiation surrounding a person or object (like the halo). The depiction of such an aura often connotes a person of particular power or holiness. Sometimes, however, it is said that all living things (including humans) and all objects manifest such an aura. Often it is held to be perceptible, whether spontaneously or with practice: such perception is at times linked with the third eye of spirituality. Kirlian photography occurs when a photographic plate is connected to a source of voltage an image is produced on the photographic plate. Basically, it's a photo of energy that is taken with the end resulting in physical colours of energy that is surrounding your body.

Anyways, nearing the end of the day most of us decided to take in a lecture about hauntings and ghosts. This guy who was doing his lecture on all his personal experience. When he started to really capture the audience with his story, he started talking about how to recognize if there are ghosts in your home. I leaned on the wall to give a listen, since I had the same interest as many there and thought that this was interesting. He began telling the audience about certain ways they make contact and how they often try to communicate with you. He also mentioned various ways ghosts try to get through by the movement of objects or whispers of your name being called out. He said that the most often sign when a ghost is present, is manipulation of lights— flickering on and off. I don't know about you, but I that there are no coincidences in our lives and that everything happens for a reason. Just as the gentlemen said that, the lights in the place went off and on like he mentioned. With gasps from the audience he seemed to gleam at the calling and requested for spirit to assist him in demonstration.

The guy then gave a pause and then attempted to communicate with this visiting spirit. Please understand that the human in me, first thought this guy a cook. He asked to have another sign if spirit was with them at that moment; the spirit obliged and the lights repeated in the same on and off fashion. More gasps and looks all around. I then looked at my buddy Michael Jackson and as he looked at me there was a realization at that moment. I swear that Mike was reading my thoughts as he tried with everything he had, not to burst out laughing as we both became aware of who the Spirit was. I wasn't just leaning on the wall but I was also on the main lights for that room. Each time I adjusted myself; I unintentionally and unknowingly was causing the lights to go off and on. Needless to say, I didn't want to get caught and we both made our way out of that place really fast. I would like to point out at this moment, that a ghost isn't always a ghost. You will learn that there are many other factors to consider before giving accreditation to a presence of either a spirit or a ghost. Whether or not people believe it, there are ghost and spirits that do exist; and they are very different from each other.

Understanding that these power trips and egos have no place while doing psychic work. If ever you find yourself on the receiving end, I suggest that you get up and leave. Another place you may see ego at large would be in some religions, politicians and authority figures. Back when you were unable to speak against the church or monarchy, there was heresy. For such actions you would be imprisoned, tortured or executed by being beheaded. Throughout these centuries, persons in a position of power have convinced many that their faith is only one; much like it is still done today. Either you must conform out of fear or follow through with the punishment as mentioned above. Understand that this was not just ego, but it was the exercising of authority to instill intimidation or fear. Today we have examples that we can use which have been part of recent history of such radical religious groups, which have used similar tactics on people. This fear fuels the authority's ego.

Just off the top of my head, I can think of a recent example—the Waco Massacre of 1993. Faith is great and so is the religion in which you have found faith, but this is applicable to those who incorporate ego. These individuals were caught up in the ego effect, where they thought they were the only ones allowed to cast down punishment. These punishments were for people, religious or not, to pray the Hail Mary accompanied by few "Our Fathers."

Here's a thought: Isn't someone who claims to be an Atheist hypocritical? If you ask someone that claims to be an Atheist what they believe in, they will tell you they believe in nothing. Maybe it's a bit of my philosophical background, but they believe they are an atheist yet state they believe in nothing. This is an ego issue. The author Neale Donald Walsh and his series of books "Conversations with God," visit this in greater detail.

I would like for you to know that it's not just religious people who think they are better then most. It is in all walks of life that people tend to think this. I think by some process of osmosis, the ego undergoes self-absorption. From my own experience, I have found that teachers, managers, psychics, priests and church congresses seem to have large egos.

Don't give up your development because someone has been telling you they don't believe you or that they think what you're doing is full of it. Just be thankful that they are not the psychic that is seeking validation or closure. As I have said and will say many times to you, this process of developing your psychic abilities takes continuous practice; which requires a thick skin. There may be times that you may not resonate with a particular person or energy, for whatever reason. As long as you can remain sincere, honest and proceed with good intentions—don't worry about what others think. I know I may have said that already but I thought it warranted repeating.

From previous experiences, one of my angels may call on you. I would do this through a reading. These readings can happen in the oddest places and can be for people whom you never thought believed in such a thing a psychic communication. With all this said regarding ego, it is a dish that is best serve unattended. We all have the ability to choose, understand and accept what brings us comfort in our lives. Who are these people to apply judgment and impose their egos and values upon us? You are who you choose to be. Do what your heart drives you to do. Become the best. Allow others to see you shine—without having an ego. Having an ego is actually an innate state, but the idea is to not focus on it. Psychic work isn't about how great you are, although you may become very reliable and accountable source by your own nature. If you allow yourself to express your true intentions, you will become a beacon of light for others to follow and seek—whether it's those in spirit or in the physical form.

By understanding the ego within you, and not ignoring it, you can learn to differentiate and keeping it in check. Always remember that self-esteem and ego are completely different and separate ideas. My aim is to try and steer you away from all the hype. This may help you understand what I personally went through and experienced. Now that you understand your ego, you are well on your way towards understanding your potential and ability as a human being and an essence.

When we allow our ego to get in the way of understanding it blocks further learning experiences. Subconsciously, it may have adverse effects by having you trying to perfect things you don't want to. Remember ego and self-esteem are both separate and important to comprehend. When you know the true intention of what it is that you are trying to accomplish, these few guidelines will help you to be well on your way.

No matter what way you look at it, this is something that must not consume the work of psychic's confidence. Confidence is gained through practice and validation with a dash of meditation. If ego is leading the psychic, then the psychic is doing unjust to other psychics who are serious about what they do. I know that this is supposed to be seen as a form of entertainment but, on the contrary, many areas such as Government and the Secret Service take this work seriously. If you ever find classes or workshops that promise a quick return for your buck, achieved in very little time then you should really investigate more about that event or psychic.

As I have said everyone is psychic. But there are those who are driven through their own ego, which includes the rich and famous factor. You may hear from some people: if it is truly a gift then why charge at all? I will tell you what I have learned. In this Universe of ours, things need to flow and exchange. That also goes for the money aspect of doing psychic work. With many jobs in our world, you need to make a living from it; this is the same for psychic abilities. Just because you charge doesn't mean that you are gouging people or ripping them off. Needless to say, this is intentionally directed to those who look to make buck at their clients expense. I have even heard of psychics using fear to accomplish their goals.

With all of this said: Are you sure you want to do this work?

CHAPTER 6

Learning to Trust Yourself

Trust, as you would have already figured out, is very important to have. Trusting yourself comes with validation and self-confidence; in addition to any other avenue that will help you attain this. For instance, take this moment and think of something you are either (A) very good at or (B) can accomplish with no effort at all. This same feeling and the end result applies toward your goal to trust in yourself. This needs to happen in order for you to become faithfully reliable with your psychic ability. I don't think that I have mentioned this, but the whole business of trusting yourself is both internal and external.

For most of my psychic development or understanding I had to learn to trust the rule of first thought. I had great issues with distinguishing between my first and second thought and how to apply myself in a situation like this. A great deal of help came from that of my understanding about trusting myself and the information I was receiving from my guides. I remember how I, much like you, often shrugged off the idea that I really do have psychic abilities? The idea is crazy right? Maybe it was a lot easier for me to understand because growing up as a kid, I had seen a lot of things that I couldn't explain. And here you are, wondering if this whole idea is just wishful thinking. You have used your abilities without even realizing it. Such psychic abilities are seen while someone is doing a reading. Notice how I didn't refer to this action as "preforming," as there is a big difference. One reason is because I personally take what I do seriously and so should you. I want you to try to remember that we're only human and not all psychics know everything; not even me. Wouldn't that be boring to know everything?

Nonetheless, you have probably already used your psychic-ness. You have probably done this while painting, writing poetry, being inspirational or even when playing an instrument. These abilities are your conscious and subconscious tapping into the world of spirituality and the universal pool of shared knowledge. This is also known as what many psychics call channelling. I speak about this on my website. An example that I can give you for receiving such information would be as follows: Can you remember the last time that you were trying to do something, such as repairing a computer, or solving an issue? Someone other than yourself, who has come from spirit, inspired those moments. This could be a complete stranger or even yourself from another time line. I would have said future but people often get weird out by that remark. Learning to trust yourself is also a process of learning to trust those in spirit, such as your guides.

This is a lot harder than you would think, as this takes practice and a combination of you, self-esteem and confidence. I think it would be wise to add a dash of validation; which never hurts. Can you remember the last time that you were trying to fix something like your computer or a program that all of a sudden disappeared? You think that it is lost forever and then you accidentally hit a key and poof, it's back—saved. Well this is an example of those in spirit helping you out. Sure there are explanations for such events, but why are we so eager to seek any excuse? Especially for a reason that isn't understood?

Such phrases like, "the answer lies right in front of you," is just that. So why is there the need to use second thought for justification? Like I have been saying, we're human. The medical field is a classic example for those people who need to justify a reason for such experiences as death. Death doesn't actually exist. By concluding that we die, you are saying that were the only life forms in the universe. We could debate this like a university philosophy class, where there is a theory to explain the correctness of the statement. But that is not what we're here for. Like I tell everyone that lends the opinionated ear, I am not here to convince you or get you to believe.

In our lives there are many instances, where our guides and angels assist us. Its all about your perspective in life, for this will finalize your outcome and reasoning towards understanding the world which is related to spirit. Through the practice of meditation and readings, you will ultimately allow more opportunities to gauge yourself as you grow along with your development. Notice I didn't say anything about accomplishments.

I don't want you to get wrapped up in this idea of having to be right all of the time; especially when you do psychic readings. As I said early on, I will be sharing my personal experiences with you throughout this book. This is in order for you to understand, that you are not the only one that will experience this. There will be others to follow in our footsteps. My hope is to provide you with the simplest and most honest help that I can by developing your psychic self. Samuel says, "This is something you cannot avoid for your own learning process."

Furthermore, be patient. You will learn this through the stages of your goals, and one day you will finally achieve it. Confidence and a number of other issues must be dealt with in order to help with the transition. Trusting yourself comes with experience, through learning. Trial and error, will pave the road of validation. Not trusting in you involves the ego.

One of the other important factors that you may need to think about at this moment is public speaking. If you do decide to do psychic readings or work, you must be able to speak to people. If you dread this, just remember to take your time. We all had to go through various related stages of our personal growth. Trusting and believing in yourself is important for a number of reasons. One of them is for the person your reading for. If you lack confidence to speak, especially when it's information from first thought then you will project this outward. That's the last thing someone wants to experience in any reading.

Let's face it, sometimes you have a bad day; we all do. Remember you are only human and seeking the guidance within (my website— theguidancewithin.com). Individuals are looking for someone, who they can see has confidence in themselves and that they posses external and internal trust. After all, they're inviting you into their lives to help them with whatever they need—within reason. When you begin to acquire traits of self-confidence you may want to journal any or all experiences you have in your development. Often times you will find messages there waiting for you in your writing. This is because you are channelling information from the spirit world whenever you write, draw, paint or sing. I would like to remind you to keep your ego in check from time to time, as it is a nice habit to get into.

Validation throughout your time of development is another good way to build on your self-confidence and self esteem. There is no better feeling then when someone comes to you for a reading and they leave with a sense of serenity, relief and validation by the words you have spoken. In all sense of the work that you will be doing, understand that whenever you are providing a reading, remain honest. If you're asked if Uncle Ted is with us, and he truly isn't then say no or state that you don't get anything. There is no shame in honesty. Both you and the client will be better off and with this you can't go wrong.

Now lets recap on a few of the things that I have said to assist you in trusting yourself. First meditate. This will always help you. This will not only help to find focus but also to focus the moment, the mind and everything around you. It allows you to focus more on the spiritual world rather than the physical. An individual working in the psychic world should possess certain qualities. The following are just a few examples: being a good listener, empathetic, sensitive, understanding and helpful. You, yourself, may want to work on these qualities. Each person is different and learns at a different rate. It is important for you not to lean on the opinion of the client—whether or not if the client liked the reading. I'm not saying don't care or don't worry about explaining anything to them. It's just that sometimes people need a bit more clarification to understand the reading.

Let the client know that not all things they want to hear will be up to their expectations. This happens a lot and you will soon learn how to deal with it and how accept it, when it does happen. Ultimately, this is assisting you to build on your self-esteem and confidence. Secondly, validate all your successes and even your failures. Use that element to adjust and move forward in your readings. You will soon comprehend that the more you learn to trust yourself, the better it is for you, your client and your confidence. These are all very important factors to consider.

Another thing to remember is that you will have people whom you are unable to connect with, for whatever reason. Always be honest and tell them. There is no sense in wasting both of your time and efforts. I still get caught up in the issue of trusting myself sometimes, as the things that I have experienced are found to come full circle. This has happened in order to help me build on my confidence and self esteem.

Bruce Lee once said: "Empty your cup, so you can fill it. Otherwise a full cup leaves no room to fill." Okay, this may have not been word for word but the idea is still there. I believe that any good psychic should pay attention to the client with the readings that take place. Remember they trust you with information in their lives that they may have not even shared with their husband or close friend. Trusting your guides is very important, especially if the information or visuals you're getting are weird. Remember the information isn't yours. As long as it makes sense to them, that's what counts. Try not to get caught up in counting the good readings from the so-called bad readings.

What I mean by those "bad readings" are the readings where the person expected something but didn't get what they wanted or that the reading wasn't as insightful as they expected. Perhaps, they flat out just didn't like it. Lets face the truth—it will and does happen. Most of the time this is a lesson to help you understand a level of learning in the experience of your development. Such as how to deal with those circumstances and how to handle the situation. Remember I did say that you will have to grow some backbone; or commonly referred to as thick skin. I will admit there were times when I did worry about this. I am proud to admit that I am glad for having experienced such. I have learned to deal with those situations in a much better way, than when I first started offering readings. But as the saying goes: "I do because I am after all human."

Personally I want everyone to have the best reading that I can offer. Therefore, I do what I can to help that come to fruition with the help of Samuel. I will make this lesson shorter by telling you as Samuel had stated it. This was said to me one day after a reading I have completed: "Any information in the readings are really none of your business. When you come to accept this and remember this then you will not have to worry if it makes any sense to you or not. After all you are just the conduit, which the information flows through. This is your role during the reading."

With that, a lesson was well learned. Remember this and it will help you out in the long run. This will help you stay away from confusion in the end of your session, so that you are not trying to make sense of the information. Whenever I catch myself, Samuel reminds me: "Ahem! Remember what I said." Just like I have said previously, all things are related and you will soon come to find out that learning is no different. To place trust in yourself involves practice, understanding and patience.

These following are the key ingredients to success:

- Be as confident as you can be, and don't rush.
- Be careful what you wish for because you just might get it! Seriously.

- When all seems lost, look within; quiet your mind, sit patiently and allow yourself to be absorbed in the energy of life.
- Understand that we are the same—entities linked to the wheel of life.
- Learn to trust yourself and the places you travel within yourself
- Don't be surprised if you feel that deja-vu sensation. This is just letting you know that you're on the right track in your life and at anytime you can change direction.

If you learn to trust yourself, then the trust will be reflective in your voice, vibration and presence. By allowing others to see the trust you have in you and your guides, they will also come to trust you. This will help with the flow of information that you will be privy to. Remember to thank them for allowing you to be part of their life for that brief moment. It is important to acknowledge this and be yourself—ever so compassionate and honest. Before you know it the experiences and years will pass, where you will have the confidence you are seeking.

Ground yourself before each reading and clear the room of any energy that is not needed. You can use any positive prayer or just ask your guides and angels to clear the air and fill it with positive energy and love. This may seem a bit weird but trust me it does work. For example, here is a simple practice that you preform. Ring a small bell or chime before and right after the reading. This first rings sets the mood and clears the energy. Negative vibrations are heavier then positive; therefore this positive chime helps to clear the air to make the ambiance lighter. You could also light a candle, preferably white or those made from bees wax. This is natural and also removes negative energy, or emotions.

Either out loud or in thought, ask the angels and guides to surround you and the person having the reading with positive pure white light. Imagine silver silk threads moving from the base of your spine and heals. Watch it move deep into the earth toward the core of the Earth, each of them attaching themselves like a spiders web. Once you picture this happening, imagine a green light of energy moving upwards along those silk threads. It goes from your feet, to your body, to your head where it is now covering your entire body. Take in a deep breath and then open your eyes and begin.

You can use the same visualization for meditating. A very quick synopsis for meditating is to sit in comfortable seated position, close your eyes and place your palms upwards. Breathe in and out slowly counting up to 10. I suggest keeping a pen and paper beside you to record any thoughts or visualizations. The concept is to allow you to get away from the outside world and pay attention to your breathing. Try not to think of anything, just allow the thoughts to happen. Do this for about (15) minutes each day.

I would like to take this opportunity to congratulate you. I congratulate you for taking this time to learn. Learning helps to cycle energy throughout the world.

CHAPTER 7

Are You Sure This Is What You Want?

Is that not a simple question? Simple enough until you have to make the decision. That decision I am referring to is the reason why you picked up this book. I feel it is necessary tell you some of the negative sides of my ability. With experience, you will come to understand and recognize the positive of psychic development. In the various pages of this book, I will pose such questions to your thought. This will help you understand what it is you want while developing your psychic ability. Everyone can do this—Yes, even you.

When you mention this interest to anyone, look around. What do you see? I get stares, under the breath remarks followed by of the rolling eyes. Others of religious faiths would attempt to instill fear into your interest, warning you about possession. Then there are others who simply think you're a little loose in the head. There are family members who would disassociate you from their lives and even disown you. There may even be friends that you lose. Are you sure you still want to do this? Of course you are. Don't allow society to generate fear of beliefs in order to conform you onto their ways.

I was baptized and raised a Catholic. Not by choice of course. This isn't really a positive way to begin life. Dictation and ethical wrong instillation of fear implanted onto you for not attending church? Wow, damnation in its best form, fear. Surprisingly to this day, these conform happen. Then here you are—myself and others alike—who choose to accept what we feel rather than what we are told to believe. Now for those running to grab stones to hurl at me, just wait a moment and allow let me say; he who is not guilty of sin, let them throw the first stone. I am not trying to create a disturbance in what brings comfort to your life, I am simply just pointing out that fear is a very well instilled program.

You are not here on this planet, to convince anyone. You are not here to make someone believe in anything, especially psychic ability. You are also not here to perform or attempt to call a spirit back from the dead. Not only is that idiotic, but its rude. You are not here to take advantage of people. You are not here to line your pockets at their own expense. This isn't about how great you are, even though in your present state you are great. This isn't about proving anything to anyone, at least not yourself. This isn't about your ego, yet it is about you. Its always about you and always will be.

Are you sure you want to do this? This is about coming to an understanding, that you fit in this place we call life; just as much as the air you breathe. This is about becoming aware of yourself and your surroundings. This is about knowing and not knowing. This is about being exactly who you are at exactly where you are; which is everywhere and anywhere.

I would like to ask something of you. Do us a favour and try no to get caught up in things. Do not begin to refer to your continuing psychic development as a great power or psychic power or something of that nature. This fuels nothing but the ego. Once you begin to fuel your ego, it may be hard to steer away from. This will ultimately leave you with a bad response or what I would like to refer to as a roadblock. Roadblock is only having the ability to apply second thought, even when trying to complete the simplest of psychic tasks. By delving into your awakening abilities, you will be invited into a world where ridicule will always be thrown your way. Remember: Thick skin.

This spiritual work is very rewarding if done with true intentions and love. Samuel once stated: "Whenever you or anyone else learns anything in life, especially when it has to do with spirituality, these actions are made for a complete learning phase. Steps are not seen as those stairs in your home or apartment, rather they are like elongated patio stones with short risers from step to step. This is because learning is not just for you but also for the experience to catch up. In actuality you designed this learning path, as you designed your life. At times it may seem more difficult, but the way in which we see ourselves in life experiencing these moments will help us to remember."

You see we all have this psychic ability, and it comes with the package of who you are just as it is written in your DNA. Some of these lessons (I am speaking from experience) are quite simple and calm, while the others seem more difficult. Remember, you're the creator of your learning and it is how you choose to do things, which matters the most. With all that has been said, are you sure that you want to do this? Are you ready to do readings for others? Are you read to develop our own personal psychic abilities?

You don't have to do anything that you don't want to. There are many awakened psychics that choose to stay out of the spotlight. Being awakened is one of the three stages as of spiritual awakening. I will explain this later on in the book. But for now, I thought I could give you some suggestions regarding development of your psychic awareness:

I.   Try to avoid doing any sort of readings if you're ill. Besides not feeling well, you may misread what is being told to you.

II.   Don't use OUJIA boards. Many people think it a game, but it is not. It may open doors and draw negative spirits into your home and life

III. Don't get caught up in reading. There is enough negativity in a person while doing a reading—you don't need to add to it.

IV. Do not make promises to conjure up a deceased loved one. Allow for them to come at their will and own time. Lots of times, clients want their deceased relative to come, but as I explain I can't make them do something against their own free will.

V. Try to avoid doing readings for someone who has just been born back into spirit or had someone in their life be born back to spirit. This is not always avoidable. But I personally want to allow grieving time. There is no time frame for grieving; as long as there are not harming themselves or their life style, who's it hurt?

VI. If you are not taking this work seriously, then stop. It is serious work that many people have placed time, effort, compassion and energy into.

VII. Avoid arguing with those who don't believe in you or the ideas that surround the psychic and paranormal world. Samuel once told me: "Your job isn't to convince anyone. Those who are skeptics are there for a reason. They already know deep inside that what you say is true. Their job is to persuade the general population otherwise."

VIII. Doing this type of work to get sexual favours from those with low self-esteem is morally and ethically wrong.

IX. If you need to ask what the wrong reasons are, then maybe you should really reconsider doing this type of work in the first place.

X. Remember credibility is yours. Accept it without ego and use it to build your self-esteem and confidence.

XI.   Remember that you won't be able to read for everyone.

XII. Remember it's not your job to convince anyone.

XIII. You're doing what you do for yourself and others who need assistance.

XIV. Understand that you don't have to take crap from anyone.

XV.   You are human and human will make mistakes—it's built into your DNA. Overcome, adapt, experience, grow and learn from your mistakes.

Again I will ask you . . . Are you sure you still want to do this?
If your answer is still yes, then I applaud you for stepping forth.
And I will say, the journey is well worth it!

CHAPTER 8

Comparison and Expectations

There is something that is gauged, whether conscious or unconscious, for first little while during the training stage. All things that will come to you are a process of training; however they may be related during this phase of training. If you haven't already compared yourself to another psychic, I would like to do that. Say: "I would like to be as great as . . ." This is nothing but a classic case of admiration. Try not to get confused and do not allow the ego to get in the way. The adjustment to your ego may be slowly delivered in life's lesson or as a size 10 spiritual boot in the behind.

When you see others who carry themselves as you do, there is a lot of confusion at first. The need to get it right and understand it all, instantaneously creeps up. But as I said, this will take time. For those who simply cannot wait, they will rush through the process and either burn themselves out or fake readings.

While developing your psychic abilities, try not to get all caught up in comparison of how good or not so good you are compared to another person. You're not alone in this process of development. This is an ever growing and understanding process. Don't believe for a moment that you are separate or singled out in the universe—we all get life lessons. Also, try to be grateful for those moments in your life that bring you validation. This type of learning continues throughout your existence as it has in many lifelines.

I know that we should love each other, tramp through the grass and holding hands while singing; just like in the movies. But our human nature and learned traits will shine though from time to time. The human side of me finds that there are those psychics that refer to themselves as being better than most. These are the people who believe that they are specially selected to be psychics. One good thing to remember, whenever you find that you are in that type of presence, is that they are experiencing life lessons just like you. In addition to that, they have to work on their individuality, self-esteem and ego. Until this has been understood and surpassed, they will repeat this process of development throughout their following lives; until they get it right. Lately I have found psychics stating that they are a true "birth psychic." I don't know what that means, but as I said, everyone was born with psychic attributes.

I admire other well-known psychics, but not because of the fame status they have attained. The last time she was visiting Hamilton, Ontario, I had a chance to meet her and her husband; they are very approachable people. I am so glad for them both they truly deserve it. The same can be said when I met and spoke with James Van Praagh. This guy has no ego and is one of the most genuine people I have ever met. There are others whom I have had the chance to speak to, although they are not as well known. Not yet at least but I admire the work they do. Their true intention is to use their own psychic abilities to help others, not so much for the fame and fortune.

I also want to mention another set of people: Lorraine Warren and the late Ed Warren. I met Lorraine in Toronto, while she was speaking at an engagement downtown. She's an awesome lady. They have assisted and continue to assist (with the help of their son) families with various conditions of hauntings and poltergeist experiences. No need to get into to too much detail. Over all the years I have been following Lorraine, I have learned that not once has anyone ever offered her a cup of coffee or something to eat, let alone a place to stay. All expenses came from their own pockets. People needed help, they are there to help and yet no one will help them. Thanks Lorraine for sharing your stories and experiences with us. She is a great example of someone to admire and aspire to be. Just keep in mind that concept of individuality. Everyone is unique and may do things differently.

The notion of comparison or comparing is such an easily nurtured trait in society. We have to reprogram ourselves not to do this as much. These two related elements are way too close to the ego and is an avenue I wish for you to avoid. Be yourself, you are unique for a reason. Yet you are apart of everything, so you don't have to feel lonely. If you want to look up those psychics I have mentioned I will place the links at the end of the book or you can beat me to it by looking them up—just type their names into Google.

Other influential psychics are Tony Stockwell, John Edwards, Rosemary Altea, Ramtha and Jerry and Ester Hicks. My intention with reading their books is to develop myself spiritually. When I first started reading their books, I was looking for validation via similar experience. Through this I would validate my personal points of experience. If you find that you're getting caught up in the comparison process, don't beat yourself up too much. Just learn to recognize it and move on. But try not to keep repeating this event. I too will catch myself doing this every once in a while. But I can say that throughout the years I have learned to recognize this quickly and to avoid it when I can. I will keep reminding you, and it is a very good to reminder, that: "We are only human." In my meditation circle each week, I am always reminding people not to get caught up in the comparison. It can have a brutal effect. Many of you will come to experience this. There is a key element and it is not to be rushed.

Another thing, worth mentioning is to try to avoid what I call, "the comparison effect." You will learn from your experience and will do things quite differently from any other psychics. You can admire them but don't get caught up in who is better as this wont help you at all. It may even cause emotions of anger or frustration.

Through the duration of the learning aspect, you will come to understand these few guidelines that are meant to help you. I know this because I personally went through this stage in my life. As I said I want to help you along the way, while giving you the tools to use at your leisure of learning. Be assured that when I have caught myself in this compare and comparison roller coaster, I tell myself change your way of thinking immediately.

My guides always remind me that this is a common learned trait in our society. It is associated with ego and the desire to be better than another. This can be manifested by achieving a higher status, no matter what the cost is. Some people would say that it feeds the soul, but I would beg to differ. I hope that my experiences will help you will grasp a better understanding, so that the transition is a little easier for you.

I would like to share a story about myself, for when I was applying for a casting call in Toronto. This was for a paranormal TV show based in Toronto. I had received a call to come and audition, so that's exactly what I did—audition. I hit the Starbucks across the road and on my way into the building I had an overwhelming sensation of walking through three feet of water. I could smell it and feel it, as I took each step in this place. Now I want to make something clear, when events such as this come up don't be surprised about the amount of people that also. Also some of the weird clothing and stares are awkward. After most of the people left it was my turn. The three or four women in a room conducted this interview.

I was told that they have a plan for a new show to air weekly and it was to do with haunted places and investigations. The spin was where a psychic and a home inspector investigated these properties. They asked their posing questions and about an hour or more onto the interview one of the girls asked: "You're the contractor right?" I mean I do workout a lot and am told that I am a solid guy . . . Oops, ego getting in the way. The interviewer continued with the question. I didn't answer and they asked again if I was the contractor? I finally said: "No, I'm the Psychic." Well they immediately turned to each other and said verbatim: "we thought you were the contractor, because you don't look like a psychic." I asked them what they expected and they alluded to someone who was an old lady or a person with a funny hat and rings on all fingers. Perhaps sporting a crystal ball in their pocket. Some expectations are often mind-boggling but it comes with the territory such as reading your mind.

At that point I asked the intention of the program and they said that they would take on submissions of reported haunted places. Then said psychic and home inspector, would go through the home and each would then give their impression or reason for activity being reported. The end result is for the viewers to make up their own mind about the outcome. I asked them what they plan on doing for those families that have issues? Or if they are searching for some sort of help? Their reply: "Why should we do anything? That's not what the program is about."

I thought during this interview from their response that, they didn't even really considered it. I would have loved to be chosen to do the show but I doubt they would have taken the whole thing seriously. Talk about an expectation, stereotype and comparison, all at it's best.

Please do not think that since you have become more awake, that you are now obligated to do a reading or perform your talents unwillingly to prove anything. You have nothing to prove to anyone but you. I have often had people who came to me for readings and times during a open conversation among celebrations have heard that comment I don't really care for which is often hurtful or derogatory.

The statement comes as this, yea I went to this other psychic and they sucked, I mean they didn't really get anything on me, or I went to a psychic and wanted to hear from my dead uncle, and they were the best cause they made sure they were there. These two statements are common and the effect is just as you read it. People have an expectation and comparison from one psychic to another. Which I admit, the human side coming out. That they all have a right to choose some psychic if they need help dealing with issues, but because their experience with a certain psychic wasn't that great and I think to myself that maybe they should really look at themselves from the readers viewpoint, I mean people often thank me for the readings with some type of statement of gratitude.

To which I am thankful, but I also remind them that it was they who did most of the work and without their input, the readings would never happen. This is true and also is the expectation of a reading which dissolution creditability from one person to another. I once was called to do a reading in Niagara Falls, Ontario, Canada. I got to this apartment and a woman from Romania answered the door and invited me in. The room was quaint for a single apartment and I sat down and we began the reading. Once I was finished, she then stated; do you not do those cards, everyone who sees a psychic knows they do those cards, I want you to do those cards. I tried to explain to her that I have not only gone over the time for the reading but that I don't usually travel with tarot cards.

She then was very frustrated, stating that she has waited for her husband to leave, (relationship issue explained in reading) and that this woman also had to lock her mother in the bedroom for privacy. Now explaining the issue with elder abuse in Canada I ended the reading and left. In case your wondering and its not a money thing here but relays the importance of getting the exchange for your work and time and travel. On the way out the door, I made sure my fee was covered before I left, and I referred another person to her who did the tarots she was looking for. This is just the first example of expectation from the client and comparison on her part with all psychics. I will say in her defense that her culture and background may have a lot to do with the end result and especially where she was from in Romania, often Gypsies were seen as the go to psychics. Expectation is a big part with any reading or involvement with the paranormal and spirit world, as well as the physical place we all live in.

We are bombarded with it everyday in our lives and are taught initially from birth. Another example of expectation is well, a little weird. I have travelled in town to a reading set up by my most gorgeous girl in the world, my wife Lezlie, who sets all my appointments. This one was in town, and at another apartment, hey I am thinking there is something here?

Well don't be surprised many lower vibrations are stuffed in these places. I went to the home of a woman who opened the door to where I thought a fire alarm had just gone off? Talk about a high pitch! This screaming child was soothed with words that weren't so nice and this seems to set the stage for the rest of this evening's reading. As I was seated in the living room, I proceeded to explain how the reading would begin as well as introducing Samuel and Sacreah, I do this with all my clients and it helps them to understand when I start talking I will be referring to someone else in the room besides them. I then proceeded to talk about her, the place and a relative in spirit who was visiting, and then there was a sense of question as to the whereabouts was her husband because at that time he wasn't in Canada.

Then there was a woman, not related who seemed to be in the picture, I can tell you this because you wont know who the client is and like I said, I am using points of reference here. The lady of the reading then jumped up and said yes, yes Dat is it (Haitian accent) Dat be da woman he fooln widt. Now with me trying to calm her down I tried my best to continue the reading and focus on other things coming up in the reading, a grandmother, anyone but she was adamant about this issue and I guess it was what she wanted to see. Well, the reading continued as best it could with her jumping up every 3 minutes to tend to the children who were screaming, and also in between her dancing in rage and waving her arms the reading was coming to a close and I was done.

Finally, I can get the bleep out of here! Ahh . . . yea . . . not so fast, This woman then asked me something I haven't heard of before and I was really taken back from it. She proceeded to tell me about the woman I have mentioned and that she knew who this lady was, and that her husband has been lying to her and is messing around while she is living here in Canada and he continues to work there and not want to follow her. (My monkey mind responded—yea blame him?) Then as I was trying to reach the door, she said this; I wont ya ta do VOODOO on em! HUH?

I tried to explain to her that wanting to do harm to another person wasn't a good idea and that maybe she either should go home and talk to him or seek marriage counseling. NO-NO she exclaimed; I know ya can do DAT, you have powers, and I won 'em ta suffer. I have to pause here and apologize, sorry buy as I am writing this, I can still hear her and am writing this way for its effect. By now I guess you get the point of the story and its comparison. I told you sometimes you don't know what your walking into and people have a expectation of you, often before you do. Now, who is the psychic? Lol.

When I think back on these moments, I have come to learn to recognize the value of those teachings that often comes from it. Whether it be to change my way of seeing something or someone, weather its race, religion or their own distinct beliefs or non beliefs. But, if I were to summarize something from all of this, I would have to say that out of those experiences which may have seemed very difficult or hard often are followed by a positive result when it comes down to it and that not all readings will be bad experiences, also they are found to be the most uplifting; for the both of you and those Spirits who decide to attend those readings.

What I have learned over these years is that, if you focus on those readings where you had a bad experience, and then you will only remember those and will eventually shy away from your study or even beliefs.

I want to share a story with you from a Buddhist monk in Australia, I think he is originally from England, he went on to explain that, while in Thailand? I think it was, there he was walking in the monastery. He then made his way down between two buildings of this red wall and noticed how nice the wall was maintained except these few bricks, which were rotted, and crumbling, each day he would walk by and see this friendly reminder. I hope to remember the story right but somewhere he realized that he was solely focusing on the issue of this wall that he forgot how beautiful the wall actually was.

After that he never saw his focus on those few discrete red brick but saw the whole wall as a great experience and admired it for what it was. My point to the story and his, I suppose he may share the same thought which is; if you focus on the negative, then you will miss the positive that is right in front of you. With this said; it is very closely related to the readings that you decide to give and if you only count the bad, that is where you will find, doubt, worry and fear. Rather see those negative readings as learning stones/steps towards your development.

Without it we couldn't judge the positive experiences and from the positive, you will find your courage and confidence, which initially came from the source of the negative to allow a point of realization. To compare and by comparison, all actions of your self, others and outcomes this is where you will find your expectations to be more rewarding and fulfilling and that the only expectation you really need is to remember to "learn lots."

CHAPTER 9

It's None of Your Business, Why Worry?

As I sit here in my office, I wonder if this title is a bit confusing to you? Actually the title couldn't have been used in a better circumstance. While doing these readings or working on your psychic development, (I thought to make up a use for the word, psychic abilities was beginning to sound too much like POWERS) lol.

You will notice that along the way, sometime or somewhere you will get it in your head that you have to worry yourself about the information that is coming through and if it at all, makes any sense to you. Consciously and from your subconscious you begin to blurt out random thoughts before realizing, that this is making no sense to you, what so ever. This is a normal thing as I have come to learn. Remember, this is about yourself and the EGO, the voice of reason, logic and what you have been told to believe or not believe in. Here I am asking you not to forget what you have learned up to re-learn in a different format.

So lets say your doing a reading for someone and that information causes you to question what you are receiving. Now, remember the rule of first thought. The information that comes from this is from whom?

Come on you remember . . . is from . . . your G, G, G, G, guides and angels. Awesome, you remembered. OK, so what if you forgot, now you know and I am sure I will be reminding you from time to time. Now the information that you are stating back to that person in the reading, seems well not to make sense? Don't worry, as I have come to learn it never does. In some cases it's like the information that comes through is often full of the monkey mind chatter from you, and filtering these messages is sometime tougher than you would think.

I often try to explain this and the best example, well, maybe not the best but the simplest and fastest way I can by stating the explanation like this; It is those spirit/guides and angels that hand me a shoe and a fork and state "here tell them this", literally. The information is presented for you to help decipher, and happens from the first rule of thought. This deciphering part I am speaking of actually implies for you to do nothing at all. Don't think about it too much or else your second thought will . . . oops, there it is again, that second thought.

There is no secret to do or not do anything in the way the information is to come. I often used to worry about what was said in my readings especially when it came to death, or a relationship, or religion. I remember some of the information that I did receive meant absolutely nothing to me but somehow the client knew exactly what it was about. This became a common thing over the years. It began to bug me so much that I started to jot down the similar readings in case one of them were beginning to think I was really nuts.

This as I said went on for a while until I heard a very familiar voice, and it was Samuel, loud and clear. He asked what was wrong and I told him that I was worried that the information I that I was getting during the readings was often not making any sense to me. I expressed that I always want to give the most honest reading to the clients and help them as much as I can.

This very moment is reminding me what he said back then . . . was to stop trying to help them. I wasn't sure what he meant then he tried to explain that my efforts during the reading and effort to make any sense of anything was not only causing me to be confused, but caused lots of frustration as he noticed in that recent time. What then am I supposed to do, if the reading . . . stop he said; "your doing it again". OK what, what am I to do? Simple he said; "nothing do nothing but transfer the information that you receive".

You are a conduit that is able to pierce the moment and see, as they cannot at this time. Besides, it's none of your business anyway, as he very nonchalantly shrugged his shoulders. I get it, and I really understood what he meant and as usual, he was right. All the while before this, I was driving myself nuts worrying about the information I was receiving, while trying to make sense of it all and just deliver the intention of the messages. Now, I am able to remember the first rule of thought and apply it. As well as, remember that any information that comes, however, so odd to me, I am to just say what I get, and not worry about what is said. As you see I have gone through this similar experience and you are not alone.

Speaking of that phrase, did you catch that I keep referring to from time to time that, your not alone . . . it's true never, even when you think your by yourself, spirit and angels and guides are always with you . . . yes even in the bathroom and in your bedroom. We are taught, as with many things in society, about this the idea of being alone or, of loneliness. It is this concept, which is instilled in each of us with fear through society, school, church and other related influences as we grow.

Along the way you will hear that phrase that "it's none of your business" which often rears in conversation with people once in a while as a gentle reminder to us all and giving us such simple signs in life were often looking for. Over the years, we seem to ignore these "tid bits" of information and run on auto-mode. I understand that you want that person(s) to have the best reading that you can provide, and as long as you do it with true intention, coming from the heart then, how can you go wrong? Now that you realize that the information that does come through from spirit is none of your business and is a polite way to help you.

What Samuel means is he would like us to stop worrying about being wrong or right; allowing the information to come through to you naturally, and be received the same way. Remember it's not about counting your success and failures in order to try to measure you by comparison.

Rather, keep in mind that this information that comes through is; really none of your business and that it is about the validation for those people who will help you much the same way you will help them. After all, without them you couldn't do the reading for them in the first place right?

I would like to mention here, as I will continue to do throughout this book for your best interest. That being said, the information that comes through you via spirit guides, angels, should be delivered with sensitivity and good verbal approach. I wouldn't want you to focus on the negative and state that their going to die tomorrow, or that someone else will. Be tactful; remember they won't forget the delivery of the message they receive, and certainly not you.

"WE ASPIRE THROUGH COURAGE AND, ENDURE THROUGH HARDSHIPS. TRIUMPH IN THE END AND, LOOK BACK ON THIS LIFE ONLY AS AN EXPERIENCE"

SAMUEL

As long as you continue on this learning curve, I guarantee that from time to time you will repeat this idea of worrying about the information or psychic impressions that you will receive. Go figure, you have to remember that there are a lot of people out there with different experiences and energies in their lives, of which you will be part of for a brief moment until they leave. Remember the information isn't yours to share with others and especially their issue or emotions, or those from spirit who are trying to get you to understand what they have gone through or feel.

Once you have become accustomed to this idea that the reading and it's information is really none of your business, then you will be able to allow the information to flow through and you will not try to dissect it as it comes, initially if you continue to do this you will lose the intention of the reading and information that may be really beneficial to that person(s), group, crowd who is needing to find closure and affirmation. You are GOD! Did you hear that GASP from many religious groups? Actually, why not. We are all made of the God source and are all a part of each other, literally. Now let me explain something . . . even though I stated that you and I and others are GOD, that doesn't give you the right or credit to proclaim to be better than anyone and being the only one to have this power.

As I have mentioned there is a real EGO and habit of many psychics that I really prefer you stay away from. Fame and glory is nice but at what price are you willing to pay for it and via the lives of others. Don't be in a hurry, take things slower and allow the whole process of your development blossom like a rose bud. Without the option reading this on your computer via a web source I will verbally add flash effect for you as this option doesn't fit on paper as it does with the opening of a web article on your computer. So for this part I will ad-lib . . . (Rose slowly blooming) ahhh . . . there, isn't that nice . . . lol

To continue, the thought about rushing the whole concept really won't do you or the recipient and that of spirit any justice. It takes a whole understanding, practice and true intention to bring this to its purpose it was made for. If you were to worry about anything, I would say that it would be best to not so much worry but be mindful when the EGO pops up, try to keep yours in check.

And remember, that you will make mistakes from time to time and will also be wonderful when you see the positive reflection on the face of your clients when they finally receive the validation and closure they have been looking for and maybe in some cases for a long time. I am glad you may be there to witness the process and help where you can.

<u>NOTE:</u> I just want to let you know that once in while Samuel and Sacreah will give their input on ideas or topics where I will put them in this book for reference for you to use.

"If it be any business that your looking to have ownership with, be it the ownership and business that you be true to yourself and to others without the rest of the junk getting in the way".

Samuel

CHAPTER 10

Asleep, Awake and Awakened

I am glad to come to this point of the book because while learning about this from Samuel and Sacreah, I can say that I have a better grasp for the reason why some people can see spirits and others can't. Actually, I often thought it was not because they can't, it's because they are just not paying attention. I will explain in greater detail about the meaning of this chapter, other wise it wouldn't make any sense now would it? People often ask this and I have also been privileged to the stupid comments made by others who seem as if I am interested in their opinion about how they don't buy any of this psychic (bad language).

Honestly, when this is said to me or in the general range of my hearing, which isn't that, great and that I am partially deaf in my left ear. Anyways, I try to interrupt them and let them be well aware that I rather not hear what they have to say. I have come to a conclusion a long time ago with the help of my siblings, I grew up with and others like them. As to why bother trying to fuel their EGO, it's not worth it, trust me. So with this said lets continue to speak about this process of being asleep, awake or awakened. As I have mentioned Samuel and Sacreah often speak to me at any time during the day or night, yes I even get awakened in the physical sense but I have to thank them because it's not often.

These processes I will refer to them as is a basic synopsis of how we can better understand as to why some people can see spirits and others can't, or in other cases do not think that they have any psychic ability at all, which you understand by now is a false sensation of understanding, by the misconception and influences of other outside factors in such as society and religions as to name a few. I have often tried to explain to people that although I can see Spirits, and they don't move like Casper on TV or howl at the moon or moan dragging chains. Well I haven't seen this, yet. (Lol) I often try to explain to people that the reason I have thought that people couldn't see was due to the fact that; people often ignore their loved ones, I will use as its often related to can communicate with us.

Firstly they were once human form themselves and have much the characteristics with them when they pass and in the physical human state if they were to come around and be ignored by you, then the same reaction would apply in their spirit form and why would they waste their effort to try to convince you that they exist if you keep ignoring them. It's a lot of work and energy on their part. I do see people as I would be looking at you and others who were more transparent, at times only making out their facial side and partial body, then wisp away. Then, there are those whom I refer to as the "grey people" or entities, I think for my sake this would be a better way for me to try to describe them for you.

They are not so nice, not like the poltergeist kind you see in the movies and I will like to say that movie's do, in this area, no justice at all for the most part. Later, I will talk more on this, which is interesting and besides I think it would be nice to share with you. Especially, since the truth is best served, at room temperature. Lets get started, for us to understand the concept of the three titles I mentioned, I would like to offer this comment before we begin any further.

For us to grasp common knowledge about all these psychic related concepts; you must understand that your entering a world that is very common and wildly known about but is salted with many forms of criticism. In the Second World War, The Cold War and Governmental Agencies; not only with Canada and the USA, but also with Russia. All have at one point or another, used psychics and their abilities to do such tasks as remote viewing, where they will draw out the vision in a particular area such as Russia for example, used as sort of a spy camera, and with these results being very closely validated by their drawings.

From World War II until the 1970s the US government occasionally funded ESP research. When the US intelligence community learned that the USSR and China were conducting ESP research, it became receptive to the idea of having its own competing PSI research program.

In 1972, Puthoff tested remote viewer INGO SWANN at SRI, and the experiment led to a visit from two employees of the CIA's Directorate of Science and Technology. The result was a $50,000 CIA-sponsored project. As research continued, the SRI team published papers in Nature, in Proceedings of the IEEE, and in the proceedings of a symposium on consciousness for the American Association for the Advancement of Science. The initial CIA-funded project was later renewed and expanded. A number of CIA officials, including John N McMahon (then the head of the Office of Technical Service and later the Agency's deputy director), became strong supporters of the program.

In the mid 1970s sponsorship by the CIA was terminated and picked up by the Air Force. In 1979, the Army's Intelligence and Security Command, which had been providing some tasking to the SRI investigators, was ordered to develop its own program by the Army's chief intelligence officer, General Ed Thompson. CIA operations officers, working from McMahon's office and other offices, also continued to provide tasking to SRI's subjects. In 1984 viewer McMoneagle was awarded a legion of merit for determining "150 essential elements of information, producing crucial and vital intelligence unavailable from any other source".

Unfortunately, the viewers' advice in the "Stargate Project" was always so unclear and non-detailed that it was never been used in any intelligence operation. Despite this, SRI scientists and remote viewers have claimed that a number of "natural" psychics were crucial in a number of intelligence operations.

The most famous claimed results from these years were the description of "a big crane" at a Soviet nuclear research facility. Joseph McMoneagle described a description of a new class of Soviet strategic submarine by a team of three viewers including McMoneagle and Rosemary Smith's location of a downed Soviet bomber in Africa. By the early 1980s numerous offices throughout the intelligence community were providing tasking to SRI's psychics, but the collaboration never resulted in useful intelligence information. Year proposed 1974.

Not to mention this type of work is recognized world wide, and is still ongoing with the use of psychics who; give assistance solving many missing persons, murder and cold cases along with police agencies, FBI and in Canada as well. I thought it important to show you even though in this present time-line of ours, these government agencies still use psychics and so do various police agencies all over the world.

So when that skeptic claims their right to debunk your efforts and beliefs, ask them to first go and convince the government to stop promoting the work that has been done for these past many years. So with that said, lets begin with the first understanding of your psychic abilities. We will title this as in order of understanding as it was taught to me, and now to you as explained by my angels/guides.

PART 1

ASLEEP

This is the process, which Samuel had explained that is the drone mode that many people all over the world reside in or choose to live. Now I am not talking about constant siesta, I am talking about the intervention of paying attention by choice, your choice, as is the same with others. To be asleep is a choice that many people find their comfort levels. It is a means by doing exactly what society dogmas as being normal, not standing out. In this mixture, people here would rather run throughout their life experiences with the normality of consistency and acceptance as a whole. This is also a place where you will find the influence of various types of dogma religions, and is also the birthplace of fear and doubt. It is a soulless place when, you don't allow your potential of understanding to grow or allow, opportunities of acceptance of possibilities.

It is a place were the fear of a non existence presence of God can be found in many forms and where is threatened through fear of persecution of not complying to, the general understanding and rules of your society and history. It is a place where the non-believers choose to reside as well as, skeptics. It is the choice of many individuals who made their decision to not get involved with any sort of abnormal behavior, which initially, this action is deemed in truth, to be in it's "abnormal behavior or abnormality". By the choice of those who rather have no interest in the possibilities of either psychic abilities or spirit involvement and firstly their choice or as you very well know the term these days, free will.

It is by these choices and influences from other sources, which perpetuate these individuals to stay in this safety zone or comfort level. This is a place where many see this thought of getting involved or having interest, goes against their religions and it's beliefs, being told that to take interest or part in this interest, that the idea is evil or that only God can accomplish such feats or powers, yes they do refer to that word as I have often heard it when I have attended church which is rare.

Too much ego if you know what I mean, besides who are they better than I and to set a set punishment or guilt by not complying. Just on that note, I was speaking to a female colleague at my other work who, one morning while discussing angels, that in church's tradition, women who are pregnant are not allowed to enter into the church, not even to accompany their family or pray. Also, her husband takes in any of their children, while she waits outside of the church. Now tell me, is that crazy and man based or what? It was a Hungarian church, and I don't mean to pass judgment but, nonetheless It is a great an example of ego in its prime!

I was wondering to myself, as often is a good thing, why would you want to be part of such a place or organization. Like I said earlier Church isn't bad and has its place but there are some cases which make me really wonder at times and if you like it great! Wow, it upset me, can you tell? Lets get away from this and continue . . . Another thought to this is that most people actual the general population are not worthy because only God can perform such feats and actions and knowing. So, to steer away from the atheist, now the Christians or like them whatever religious dogma, God created everything on earth right?

Right, lets not forget that we are often told that he is a vengeful and fearful male God, and punishes us severely in purgatory. We should not forget that only a priest or a reverend could forgive on mother/father

God's behalf? Do you see the pattern here, it's man made, man based, for influencing control, fear and doubt.

I think that much like the ego factor if you find a religious person who teaches from his faith and heart, away from his own ego, then like psychic work . . . this is where you should focus your attention and faith. There it goes again, my monkey mind. I can't guarantee to steer away from these inputs to thoughts but I will try to keep them to a minimum. I apologize, Samuel wants to continue . . .

In many cases, it is often taught that the idea of us angels, are even seen as a devils tool used to fool the general public and, that we never have any direct relation to helping man or woman kind, let alone speak or talk to God our "father and mother, the alpha and the omega." To you, we ask to search deep inside your being; do you think this to be true? Of course not. We are always around. Through our own assignments or charges we work and also assist you and many others daily by your own request if needed. We also assist by guidance as well as, working to help exercise your right to freewill, which by is universal and God's law. We are not meant to intervene without request or order of universal law and flow of life and your growth. It's sort of like the "prime directive", on your fantasy television series called Star Trek. So, there it is, the explanation of being ASLEEP. It is being state of being which is constant, conscious and subconscious. Instilled by uncertainty and fear, fueled by doubt; a good example of atheism and non-involvement by freewill.

PART 2

AWAKE

By this process of your understanding we have given title to these usages of reference to help keep the explanation and understanding as simple as possible for all. Unlike the previous mention of being asleep, this here is almost it's opposite. Here we find that many have a spark of adventure towards possibilities, which were not instilled by your education institutions, well until the last few years that is. Now a day you can find many spiritual schools that teach about metaphysics, paranormal and other healing work such as hand on healing or lying of hands. Many refer to this as reki practice and for some reason, people have added levels to gear payment to the study and all actuality, levels really don't mean anything. As is such humans are much connected to attachments and also are convinced that unless you pay more or are rated higher than another in whatever the subject, unless this is attained there lays no value to the outcome result to give various levels of acceptance or validation.

"It's all the same really". Now we are not saying that those validated at a level seven or reki master level does not mean are not worthless its just the fact that all of you have very much these similar attributes of such ways of healing and psychic abilities. We are simply pointing out that often times, society gets caught up in the idea that, paying more for such as services, is better or that a higher whatever it may be/degree is better and simply is not the case. Just look at those countries, which do not have as much on your side of the planet and live each day as it is the last. They too, use what you call the "healing hands", and are paid next to nothing and, often not at all, in order to help another human being as much as they can just because they want to remove the suffering or simple ache.

Your kind, sometimes refer to them as witch doctors or medicine men, a term which loosely represents its true, intention. Society has taught you this way of judging worth and value of such examples and has been conditioned all throughout your lifetimes; it separates those that have and those that have not. Ask most wealthy people; if you were to give up all the money you have, and start over, by making a minimum wage, would you do it? Their reply will get you a twitched eye, followed by are you kidding? We will tell you that there is enough for everyone on your planet and in your world to have the same, but it is because of the action of those who have everything want to keep it that way in society and assist to continue to create this and add value, cost to all things. We will like to tell you that there is no money in heaven, and do you want to know why?

It's because you come to realize you don't need this attachment, and that everyone can have anything at any time. Ultimately, if your world/generation can remove the need for want, there would be none who would go without. On this note, there are teachers out there, who would like to assist you, if you so wish, who have learned this knowledge of such healing of hands and other healing and psychic practices, we are simply reminding you to not get caught up in the process of allowing the EGO get in the way of your learning. You are already masters in everything you do, believing it, is where your journey takes you.

Samuel/Sacreah "Now, we will explain the process of being awake" . . .

"As we mentioned, more and more of your planet is becoming aware of this awake process of understanding, which elates us completely with joy; and that is because you are finally paying attention to those Spirits around you, along with your Guides and Angels. Even if, it uncertainty followed by curiosity. This action alone, moves the energy in the universe of creation and also the energy around all things especially, you. By being aware or as some of your Buddhist teachers would express, you are being/becoming in the state of mindfulness. 'Aware' or, as we explained it to Gordon, you are becoming AWAKE."

By being "AWAKE", this is a developing process that grows with positive energy, each moment you experience as positive has an effect on the whole process, its like fine tuning a car, the more you care for it and pay attention to it, the more you become aware of its workings, and is such as the state of being "AWAKE". This also comes and is refereed to the experience those and even you may have had that relates to a Psychic or some sort of Paranormal event.

You may have been living in a home or staying somewhere and your experience may be such as to hear your name being called, by other than a physical person or audio device. Spirits who wish to communicate will often pick those individuals whose minds are not busy due to their concentration on another item at that precise moment. They may find that by moving an object such as your keys or even moving a glass across the position of a table to spark your attention. Such experiences, relate to what we are referring to as this process of being AWAKE, by having an experience of some sort to cause you to wonder about the possibilities or even having experiencing an event that validates; in some way for you to become a believer, or at least not snarl at the idea that there is another world, spirits, guides or ghost and yes even psychic ability.

To those who choose to pay attention, eventually move onto the next process that we will now refer to as being; AWAKENED.

"In the process of the information that your mind generates there lies deep within the heart beat of knowledge and it is by this emotional understanding where you may find your belief, faith or truth in your life, try not to walk around with hose blinders on and you will often surprise yourself of what you already knew in the first place."

Sacreah

PART 3

AWAKENED

In this final phase, I will speak about the process of human recognition and perception and it's status in your life as well as others. I will speak on that moment of recognition, of clarity. Not with your eyes rather with your moment of realization of the spirit world including guides and angels, not to forget those other little helpers we call pets. This is all realized through your personal experience, sometimes on more than one basis. As I have been told, this is the final stage of the three-stated process of recognition or knowledge of the spirit world and it's existence.

From what we have noticed over the years, often those who are in the first stage of the ASLEEP phase, it's not until they have some sort of validation or involvement/experience that they will even move toward the second phase and some all the way to the third stage were speaking about. Although we all have psychic abilities that, we are born with, many of us are taught, not told, that this idea doesn't exist or is easily dismissed as a simple child's play by our parents from of our early experience. As children we often talk about those in spirits especially in our early physical stage of our development (baby stage). When we get a little older from the toddler stage we play with friends that are not there to the adult world and are easily dismissed.

As we grow we learn to accept this false sense of perception and eventually become non-believers or atheist. Some, may be lucky enough to decide their birth and life will start with a family who embraces and values these experience and beliefs or in some other cases possibilities and as I said other will not, due to their (non) beliefs, faith, or, other ways of interpretation from society's viewpoint. Even though we are coming of age in our time that this idea of ghost, the spirit world and angels and guides are becoming more accepted but there are still those who prefer not to talk about it at all, for reasons I have mentioned earlier. Look for my reference about fear and religions in the previous paragraphs. It is often the teaching through religions ; I don't mean as to seem that I am attacking a particular faith or belief you may have, and is really not my intention. Not all religious faiths are alike nor, is one better then others.

It's just in some cases, there are those who idea's seem a little too far fetched and is based on producing guilt or fear. There are some churches, which require you to give them a percentage of money you make each month or paycheck in order to be in a better place with God.

Neither mother Azna nor father God, don't care how much money you give the church and in fact they rather if you give it away then, give to the needy or your neighbor. At the end result, if it's what you like then, what the hell right and as they say to each there own. When we become AWAKENED it is this stage that we have a experience where we have come to understand that we can and have communicated with spirit, guides and angels.

Our experience can and do vary from person to person and is this way because where they are in their lives, those who choose to remain ASLEEP, do so from their own choice, even if it is influenced by another. Have you ever tried swimming against the current? It's really hard as I said I will give personal experiences and swimming in the Niagara River, from jumping off at the bottom of the peace bridge in Fort Erie is not only a stupid youthful idea, it's damn cold under the bridge and well . . . let me tell you, everything shrinks and when its time to swim to shore, that current your swimming against to get there is very difficult at times, and in relation by example; so is attempting to do any psychic work and as I have mentioned if you stick with it, you will eventually over come it. The difference here is that there is no shrinkage to worry about . . . lol

This part really doesn't need any elongated explanation, it describes the finale stage or phase about understanding the process of those who have moved towards another area of their understanding and that there is more to our world than just us. By becoming AWAKENED, most people usually have had some sort of experiences, which, in turn has influenced the way they feel or understand about the spirit world or even psychic development. There are other possibilities that may be related such as, other life forms and planets.

Often at this stage, people will often find that they have experiences similar to many others and given the fact that like minds attract, they will undoubtedly find others of a similar interest, or, in some cases, may have even joined a meditation circle in their area . . . This is a hint to you, and wouldn't be a bad place to start. Regardless at this phase of being awakened, people are often communicating and experiencing the spirit world on their own or with others and from this you and they are well on the way to seeing life in a very different light, excuse the pun.

"It is through trial and error in your thinking that will allow for much growth depending on the outcome of your thought. Recently people have been paying attention to this from known sources and they in turn are teaching others no matter how insignificant the end result is or without their knowledge. Your greatest gift is to do for yourself so that you can do for others and if your choice is not to do anything, then blame only the end result for your life experience and stop wondering why you feel as if you have to repeat the process of things in your life. When you realize the lessons and that you have finally learned then your mind becomes aware and awakened that not only that

you have greater potentials, but that you now see the world in a difference of radiation and your life with a better experience by allowing yourself to become awakened".

Solis (Non Angelic, Spirit guide)

CHAPTER 11

Readings for Seniors

Here is a place where I bet you have never given consideration for readings and I never gave it any thought to tell you the truth myself. But none the less we are here and you are there either standing or reading, I'm psychic not a mind reader, so stating you thought I would know is beyond the point . . . lol During my experiences doing readings for a lot of people over the years I am always amazed how things change from reading to reading and I am referring to my own personal growth.

When ever I do readings, I learn about dealing with a certain ethnic group of people and see things in a different perspective, not being racist, but I have had the opportunity of dealing with someone from Haiti while doing counseling at the Salvation Army, and that person demanded that she get everything handed to her and was her right, well not to make the happening draw out I will say that because of her, as I am also human I was left with a different thought about everyone from that place who is coming into Canada as a refugee. Lets us say she was not a nice person.

But I will tell you that your teachers who will often help you in growth and experience in your life will be this sort of person until, you learn whatever it is and are able to move on as I have, OK so it still bugs me from time to time, not the woman just people who come into the country and won't abide by out traditions and values, but lets leave that for another lengthy. Allow me to continue, during your duration of continuous learning about self, you will learn how to deal with the emotions, beliefs and non-beliefs and from all ages, well at least I thought so until that day.

My wife, Lezlie who usually books all my appointments and is my director for those who decide they would like to have a deep trance channeling session with Samuel or Sacreah which people may to speak directly to my guides. On this reading, which is refereed as an open reading where I am the conduit between both worlds, has booked me an appointment through a good friend, who's mother wanted to see me for a reading. No worries as I stated to my wife. Just let me know where it is and when to be there? Well our friend Ginette Hunter who is a great "Feng Shui Consultant", and who is on the website in Ontario, had a friend Nancy who, booked this appointment for her mother.

Lezlie said; I have an appointment and it is in the Falls (Niagara Falls, Ontario, Canada) and that she is well . . . Um . . . is in her late 80, early 90's.

I was always curious as to what I could ever tell someone of that age? Well the angels and guides, as I feel to this day had a hand in this. Well, my first thought and reaction was, human and followed my initial reaction, which was . . . what the hell can I tell her that she hasn't been through or already know?

Mainly most of my readings ranged in age from 18 to late 50' s at best and very rarely 80 years old. So with this reading now scheduled four days away, each day I kept wondering what I am going to tell this lady, at the same time I began to worry about the outcome. Two days later, I started to wonder if should cancel the reading, and that I can say that I was actually regretting the reading before it started. All day long as I was going through in my mind over and over trying to find a reason not to go and trying to figure out, what exactly could I even tell her let alone where would I begin? I also had a thought that this lady had probably been around when the Titanic sunk, and funny enough, I later found out that she was.

Well, I finally grew a backbone and decided to go to do this reading, which was scheduled in the Falls. (Niagara Falls aka Southern Ontario, Canada) much to Samuel constant reminders that; there is a reason and that I will find out why it is so important when I'm done, and also not to worry.

Sure, easy enough for him to say but as Samuel often does, he keeps assuring me that everything is all right. I remember wondering during that day if the reading may have been was a question regarding the time she had left here on this earth, and the I reached my destination and the thought left as quickly as it had arrived. I arrived a little before seven to a very nice retirement home, or I think the proper term would be adult lifestyle community centre. This place at first glance, looked as if a bunch of Victorian houses were mashed all together by a hurricane, and the end result was an amazing feat of architecture and balconies.

In the entrance to the hallway, I was buzzed in, and down the hall I went, where a beautiful lady received me, with a very youthful energy in her eyes and a hidden treasure story about her life. I was actually surprised just how spacious and nice it was. As she motioned me to sit, she continued to gather herself and some items for the reading. While that was happening, my monkey mind visited and I found myself wondering about those who lived in this place and watched me as I made my destination and imagined that they were trying to guess as to who I was, some guessing I was her grandson/son coming for a visit.

As I played with this thought Samuel busted in and said maybe she told them why, you were there already with a sinister chuckle. As with small communities, word of mouth gets around really fast I thought and decided to let this go as she returned seated herself and the reading began. This lady sat beside me and introduced herself, as I did the same, we seem to have hit it off as if we were long lost buddies. I heard stories about her life and experiences that would have made a great book. As the reading went on I was given validation and she had expressed that many times in her life she has had psychic experiences and in her time as she called it, it wasn't something you would talk about. I know your waiting for something to stand out resulting from this reading and as I tell everyone, the readings are something that isn't shared.

Especially at the request of this woman who still has children living. I will say that she said she had a great time with her life here and had no fear of what was to come next by leaving this life. She actually made me feel so very comfortable that with the reading completed, we kept talking for a few hours before I realized how late it was.

She inquired about my idea of a book at that time and I told her that I was beginning to work on one but was far from completion. After stating she would like to read it, and given the circumstance, I know she is reading over my shoulder as I write this book and also promised that she would be the first to be allowed to read my rough draft. So with all this now finished, I thanked her and made my way out until I realized that I was LOCKED in the building. After waiting for security to question me about why I was there so late, I said I was visiting and lost track of time. Once I was outside and in the car, I was overcome with a great giddy feeling of happiness and then, there it was . . . Samuel s voice.

Saying, you see everything is all right, and now you have another part to add for your book. That is why you were directed to go there specifically to do a reading for her. In order to have the experience of reading for someone who is in his or her late years of life. Learning again, to just allow the information to come and enjoy yourself. She on the other hand, had previously asked aloud/ actually wished for someone whom that she could talk to and let out all that information she spoke to you about, and to confirm she wasn't crazy. As well as, to experience laughter/unconditional acceptance from a stranger. It was a good fit and was also for the purpose of this book, that will help others to realize that readings are not gender specific, age specific or environmentally specific, it is what it is and will be, world without end and with that I went home.

I can say that it was enlightening and continues to be for me, regarding my personal understanding and growth of my psychic development. Not to be confused that one day it will end, for reference refer, to the previous chapters I wrote about on the three processes known as, Asleep, Awake and Awakened. Learning about this development if I haven't mentioned prior is like steps that are elongated rather than narrow like those in your home, this is due to the time-frame that exist with each personal growth, until it is time for you to move forward into the next stages; all depending on you of course! I can honestly say that I haven't topped this type of experience of my reading in a long time and is much like that I would relate to the experience as a native traditional sweat-loge, or snowflake and the reason is simply because, no two are alike.

I may have been close on a few occasions such as the times I met, spoke and worked for other psychics such as, "Sylvia Brown or Psychic Medium, James Van Praagh" in Toronto who, when I attended one of his shows with my wife and friends, had all those attending, do a psychometry readings for complete stranger's. This is done by reading the psychic impression from an object that a person is wearing or, which had belonged to someone. Even with those who have been passed? Remember, everything has energy and like fingerprints does leave traces behind or with an object or item.

James had asked me to talk to the audience which was great because it not only help me with this experience but, also allowed for me to meet James as, I always wanted to when I was younger. Awesome, well at least I thought so! What can I say; some people have superman or batman as hero's and I have people who do the psychic work that I really admire. Maybe to help you recognize who he is, he is the guy who produced the idea of the television series called; Ghost Whisperer starring, Jennifer Love Hewitt or just Google him he does have his own website as does Sylvia Brown. From that time on, I can honestly say that I have continued to read for much older folks than I and as I have mentioned earlier none much younger than 18 years of age, unless really necessary, which isn't often.

So when if you do find yourself in a similar experience just remember, that your guides and the universe are constantly working in your favor and will continue throughout your existence in this life and into the next.

CHAPTER 12

The Building Steps
Towards Learning – Q&A

Remember those stairs I was referring to earlier? Well I would like to start off by telling you to 'get used to them'', and their wonderful adventures which, you will experience through out your life teachings in order to assist you with this interest of your personal psychic development. As I have mentioned the learning steps that I often refer to while teaching psychic development in our home is given the physical example of sets of stairs leading up a mountain side. These steps are not steep, but rather they are elongated, meaning that once you begin to experience each step; you will come to learn about a stage in the development of your psychic abilities, whatever they may be? Also as I have mentioned reach person is unique and will develop in other ways or similar ways such as yourself.

These steps, which I don't want you to become too concerned about are, steps, with each their own purpose for that point in your life. This happens a lot in order to assist you to understand what it is that at this moment, help you grow in your awareness and psychic development through your life experience. Sure life will give you an experience whenever it comes along, but for this purpose and clarification at this moment, this is a bit more specific and is geared/directed to assist solely on you and your development. As always, try not to be in too much of a rush to complete each step. Remember that saying "patience is a Virtue? It is a true fact. Being in a hurry and rushing this learning experience/ process can have its effects which may create a road block for yourself and we or rather I prefer this not to happen to you. By just allowing whatever it is happen, the flow is more fluid and natural which, can be easily recognized and understood by you when each change is to come and believe me you will learn to recognize this process of change and development.

I can personally say that I not only have experienced this but when it does take effect, this energy sometimes can leave with a sense that is at the same time, a bit overwhelming and exciting and, leaving me feeling full of energy and restless. These steps, which I am, referring to, can and will come at its own pace. When you are truly ready, you will move on and learn to accept the change and how to deal with it. Eventually, you may even help others seeking the same path as yourself. Is there an end to the learning?

I would like to tell you "no" then again, there could be an end to it all especially if you decide this is something you rather not do at any point in your life. It is your decision where you go and what you do with your "Psychic Tuning". You see there it is; you're already advancing in our usage and reference to the words "ability or development".

Meaning, by now you should already understand the process about "learning lots", and are well on your way since beginning to read the first page of this book. Did I tell you there is magic in this book, and it can be seen when you realize that you have an attune that carries on the process of understanding the spirit world and all life around you, there is an unspoken broken silence in the universe in and around you.

I wanted to share with you a quick story of something that relates to asking for something from the universe. I attended a Sylvia Brown conference in Toronto a I actually think it was my first one. It was amazing time and was great to see her, as like many other people had seen her on Montel Williams-talk show. Well I had made a wish to the universe, actually a request to have an opportunity to sit and speak with Sylvia Brown, at least an hour or so, not to ask for a reading but to, just talk. Well time went by and at this part in my life I was looking for a job and was called to an interview at a gym as a trainer. Well the interview was great and lasted for roughly 45 minutes, at the end we exchanged business cards as is something I always did, instead it was a general contact card with name address etc. As I got into my car I quickly glanced at her card and it read, SYLVIA BROWN—Physical training Manager. What a hoot I tell you really, be careful what you ask because the universe does have a sense of humor. I didn't find it too funny but taught me to be more specific with my requests in the future.

On your building steps towards your learning try not to be in too much of a hurry, as you will burn yourself out and lose out on a lot of very important lessons along the way. You see when learning about your development you learn in steps, not like the stairs in your home but more like long patio steps, due to the time each step will take you, and if you think short cuts will help, trust me you will learn very quickly to take this slow. This also allows for you to better understand the experiences that you are to learn with each step. Then there will be time when you can become to recognize when these lessons are to change by the ending of the current lesson and heading towards the other. Trust me its worth the wait.

I can attest to personal experience that, I have seen, and know of some psychic's and channeler(s) who rushed this building steps towards learning, and skipped the lesson's required for themselves just to see how great and powerful they are. And who will eventually fall into the category of charlatans. Caring for their own benefit along the way. Each person as I have mentioned learns at his or her own pace and for good reason. To those who wish to rush, I will ask them to find something else to do like politics, at least you will be in the same field, and that way people can expect what they get in the end. I'm getting off topic. Just remember that those lessons that you will learn are a "life time" of lessons. There is no number to say you are done, and have completed all you need to learn. That's why the angels tell us that were here to learn lots!

Samuel is telling me that; it would be a good idea at this time in the book to add some questions that you may have, and that the Angels will assist in answering to the best of their ability to our understanding.

Can I choose my own lessons to help me speed up my psychic attunement, and if not, what about my freewill?

Actually no, this is nothing about choosing over a freewill decision. This is about developing your mind and learning to understand at, your level of spiritual maturity to where you are at this very point in your lifeline. You are correct if the point of argument in understanding that you can do the opposite as; free will is yours and by attempting this you will gain EGO, by skipping each phase of spiritual understandings., but along the way, you will come to learn that there will be pieces that will be missed which are of great imports.

Is it true that those who wish to study the guidance within can only do so by help of another person or psychic?

During these stages on my own attunement of my psychic development, understanding and growth. I had learned to tell when, the teachings in these steps have changed, at the moment it begins. But seldom, do I see the end results until the lesson is complete. This is because of the fact that if we already were aware of what it happening we wouldn't pay very much attention to whatever that lesson may be and miss the whole concept of this phase in understanding where we are in our lives in order to help ourselves as well as, others in our beautiful blue planet. I will tell you to be careful and take each step slowly and allow the transition to come along all on it's own.

Take each step as it comes and to clear this understanding for you a little bit more, look at it this way. You have an interest at this moment to do more or find a way to do more to strengthen your understanding of your psychic awareness, once you have that bug (we will call it that for lack of words) of getting excited and having the people or situations that come into your life that will leave you with validation of some sort. When this goes on for a while it will become second nature. At this point you will become more confident and understand this learning phase without doubt, the next step towards learning will then come on all on it's own. Each step different as I have mentioned from the beginning of this book.

Is there risk involved with delving into this experience or subject?

With anything, your world will state that with everything, there is a risk. To what extent were not so sure, only because the only risk is that, which you create.Remember thought creates action and, can manifest itself given, enough focus, concentration and energy. It is the understanding that such word or wordings used such as this one you refer to as "risk" and, that will lead into the instilled or your society and those in power positions to place a belief of fear and if there is no fear on your part of learning what you already know then, your answer is "No".

Can another psychic steal "my", psychic abilities?

No one can steal this from you. Understand that it is part of you as, the organism you are combined with. There are those whom you may caution of being as termed "psychic vampires" a humorous indication of Charles Dickens meats Jaws. Meaning, this is a very descriptive visual tool to have and find those seeking to find and watch out for someone of a intentional glare of intimidation with long fangs and a cloak. Far be it from us, to intervene of your freewill and imagination but again this exists because those who are described by others as psychic vampires" are those individuals who prefer to remain bleak in their experience in life and outlook to mankind and especially their circumstance. This is in reference to those who do this, not to those who speak of it or try to help you and others to avoid it or the experience and how to recognize it and remove it from your person and spirit. These sorts of people seem to drain the energy from you and when they leave you feel irritate, restless and angry or upset. Now you can choose to experience psychic phenomenon and then ignore it completely.

This sensation and your own freewill of choice would be what you would be referring to as "someone stealing your psychic understanding or ability or attunement" away it is ultimately "you" that can only do this, its about choice, thoughts become action, so choose good ones.

What if I don't like what I see during psychic readings?

Well with this, we will state that you can ask for assistance and or buffers to not allow so much detail to be transferred. By seeing the outcome of an event such as a tragic accident, allows you to fully understand the sincerity of the impression you are receiving in order to give a persuasive and accurate reading for that person or yourself in order to properly understand. We think the quest of your question should be directed more towards asking if you can filter out what you don't want and the answer is yes, you have what we will term to your understanding "control." Which in itself is an illusion because it is never attainable and if stilled eventually you will loose it again repeating the same process to try to have it.

Let what happens, happen naturally this is the closest to control that you may actually come to by not doing anything at all, and it's not a materialistic object you give yourselves in order to determine its title to be "mine." In the end doing this type of work in your world, you may be privy to seeing what you do not want, and we say that when it does arrive as your experience, understand that this experience or visualization is not yours just as the pictures on your television are not yours, you just simply change the channel and, this is much the same.

If while giving a reading as an example we will perform, experience physical pain from another who is trying to impress upon you their experience's in their last lifetime. When this does occur, simply tell them to back off and slow down or find another way to communicate. Remember they want to help you to communicate as much as you want to help them with their family or whom-ever. Even if its just to understand their experience so they can leave it from their memory with your help, and also to allow them and those to move on.

By doing psychic readings or getting involved in this area of interest; can I attract other mean Spirits?

Understand, that when you delve into the world of the spirit you will likely pick up on those spirits who can be negative or others, given their life experience before their passing. It may be that the intention of you be true and honest but you must also know that their vibrations and vibratory fields that you will come in contact with in one way of another.

What we mean is those negative spirits revolve around a much heavier and lower vibration than where you exist. If you delve into the negativity of the occult as you know it, yes you can attract energy that you don't want or may not understand. As with everything you know of there is an opposite of everything. Remember this, you are never alone and we are always with you, when you need our assistance. As you term the expression, becoming psychic, you are not only becoming awake or awakened depending on your state of understanding, you are none the less a light in the dark and curiosity has it's place. This is why it is very important to ground and protect yourself.

By this we explain this process as almost placing on a winter jacket wrapped with the brightest light of God, and ground yourselves in order to help balance the life force within and around you. Your mind is such a magnificent tool and you also can conjure up your fears if you allow it. Energy exist within everything and is whether, it is still or not, silent or not, living or not, in all places at all times. If you concentrate and focus on the negative that has been taught and ingrained to you from your parents to theirs and so on and so on as well as those you deem as your authority figures, fear will do its part and assist your thoughts to become what it may.

Those spirits whom have crossed, over as you understand the term or as Gordon has explained, it is born into, do not stay in homes decrepit or new just to make moaning noises in the dark while, floating inside bed sheets. They do, however, learn to associate the impossibilities and possibilities, which allow them to communicate in some way they learn how and that you can recognize. Whether it's through another medium, or other choice of avenue to communication. Your television and movies do no justice to the existence here and is waved off to even think of the possibility by others, as is negative entities created by thought. Ghost much different than Spirit are those essences, which are for some reason or another afraid to cross through guilt, anger disbelieve and fear.

Sometimes a tragic event will leave them in a frozen time of their mental state and lock them in a disillusioned place of existence. In its actuality, it's just that tunnel with the light to which many of you refer to when making your way back home/heaven. Either way, they eventually make it with some help.

To answer your question, by practicing to develop your psychic side or inside of you this depends on what you experience via thought. If you want to experience them they will oblige you. Just understand that it takes a strongly developed soul essence to deal with this type of energy. Once your ready you will know what to do, when to do it and how to do it. Where, depends all on the moment".

Samuel has a question for you;

How can you tell, if what you are here to do is what you want to learn out of this lesson here in your life? Before you realize of those unaccomplished options and experiences, if led by another to dictate of your time and experience through their will and not of your own. If so misunderstood about your path in your life, and that you must go somewhere to find yourself, we say look at your feet and there you are. If you were to look into the mirror we would say there you were for time is but a split moment into thought towards the action of change and growth. Base your experience in life not led by another or governmental yoke, experience what you may at your best and that for the best of others, for it has been said that which you do onto my brothers, you do onto me.

How can I tell if I am ready to do readings for another person or communicate with Spirit?

We would say; by reading the pages in this book, you already are. You are, at this moment, listening as you read with your minds thought or, voice to the words as they are transcribed by Gordon to you through us, as "we" are speaking; meaning I Samuel, and I Sacreah.

You can clearly tell when you ready to communicate with Spirit the moment you do just that, by speaking aloud or quietly in your mind to a loved one. The moment they hear their name they hear your voice. Unfortunately by being here in the physical sense, you have to learn to filter out all the outside and inside noises such, as your own thought.

Your intention and desire to communicate may take some practice and often people will state to Gordon that they have heard a voice call their name, clearly heard their sister speak to them just before they woke up from sleep. There is no degree or certificate that comes with this and if you find that you are challenged by others who state, that you must have such a decree of authorization, tell them . . . God sent you!

For we, would like to remind you that, you are God within that entire existent of the universe, a source from existence, with this said, how else would you be where you are, there are no coincidences, everything does and will happen for a reason, it's the universal law.

How do I deal with those who don't believe in my psychic abilities?

Samuel speaks . . .

We would ask in difference to the question as this . . . who are they to demand proof that what you experience is real or not?

You are charged with no purpose to make anyone understand or believe in you or that of your psychic abilities of any sort and even the existence of we, or that of the Mother/Father God. Your present moment is a gift, and we would like take on this moment and quote from the known author "Neil \Donald Walsh" of his series known as "Conversation with God" . . . it is that this known "present moment" which, is a true gift from God given unto all and is why it is called "the present". Freewill, yours to explore and grow and learn from as best as you can and if this is that you believe in yourself, then there is no worth in boosting or bloating your EGO for another interest or purpose. Take credit when given but accept with no EGO, rather accept this with gratitude and knowledge you have helped another human being bring comfort onto them. That's what matters most, so think unto this not, as it will occupy your mind in a constant reminder.

It is best left undisturbed for doubters to handle to themselves. To demand proof of yourself is to question your own validity of source, it comes from you from within you, through you and, around you. It is, the faith that lies within your rooted understanding and known knowledge that; which has always been in existence since the source of life and into this world you are in. We will elaborate more in the other book that is to come.

Does meditation, really help with my psychic development?

Actually yes, it's scientifically, and psychologically proven. The reason for this is because it is, the process and practice towards learning to breath, and quiets your thoughts. Which allows for the development of your own awareness around you and within yourself. It also helps you towards more such developments of awareness and the ability to listen to the subconscious mind in order to assist you to focus on the vibrations on the present moment, that comes from the thought of your guides and angels.

We would also like to add in addition to this answer, do not be hard on yourself if you forget from time to time, as with most things in your world life does and will go on and often times, get in your way. Automatic writing is also a good avenue to use if you cannot meditate quietly with your eyes closed, though there are other forms of such meditation that also takes no effort such as, walking in nature, be silent, observe and listen. You just, may be surprised what you experience?

If everyone is born with psychic abilities, how come we all are either not aware or do this on a daily basis?

The answer is simply because, the choice is and has always been yours. Actually very few of your people, meaning species ever do decide to venture into remembering this or that, they even want to desire to do so. This is where you would find your atheist and others alike who prefer to remain asleep. (This is spoken about in the beginning of the book, so if you flipped to this then look there for reference.) You all have freewill and each person has come here to experience their lives that are difference from others, in order to develop their spiritual awareness, where some others are not yet ready to move forward.

Then there are others who have come into this world time and returned again who, are already aware of their spirituality, such as the Dali Lama, in order to help teach others and repeat this cycle until all are aware of it and that they have always had it. The psychic spirituality and knowing of life and the universe. There may be more that you will undoubtedly think of but at this present time we see it as sufficient for the purpose of your understanding and know that questions are never ended in its quest, when searching for the conclusion, make your quest most important. Here we have supplied a few questions we thought to reply to, before you had asked and that there will be more added for another place and time.

From one of my Spirit Guides;

Your road towards your learning is, a road travelled not by many and to those few who choose to, not daring themselves for their own purpose of ego but do so, in order to help others. It is by these intentions', which is within their nature to do so. Doing for themselves to help others.

Does so, to help themselves in this learning and development in their own experiences. Choose wisely and honestly with your heart and you will find that the rewards outweigh the medium of exchange of coins, which in itself, it is another reward to your spirit. Always remember that the exchange of energy is needed and if to make a living by following your heart is the best place to launch from this is as good as any to begin.

CHAPTER 13

The Psychic and The Ghost

A lot can be said for the work one does using their developed ability, talents or what you want to describe what everyone else can do as such? Lets talk about the work done using your psychic talents to help another.

Now the general public who is unaware does not understand and sometimes I often wonder why they can't comprehend that not all psychics are alike. Were not the "Borg" for those who don't know, they were on a television series of Star Trek created by the spin off of the original series by Gene Roddenberry. Their take on existence was based on assimilation of all races to their own; basically they would add your race with the collective to be linked as one. Great show and, fantastic idea by what I describe Mr. Roddenberry as a modern day profit in his own right and time. Not to get off topic, but if your to watch the older versions into the new ones you will see ideas that compose of the cell phone, ear phone, ipad and others of similarity, maybe it was a sign of the times in what was to come but none the less it's present today that was never thought of existence accept on television. Can't wait to see what they can do with teleportation . . . lol

In any case as we said; all psychics are not alike, they made do work in similar fashions but remember the EGO factor and is always a good sign to be weary. I have had and, have learned a few days ago from a reading that I did about two weeks today that someone at the reading/ party when there is more than 5 people as it is refereed to as, wasn't satisfied with the outcome of the reading. When I heard of this I was SHOCKED! OK . . . so I really wasn't. As I said earlier in the book, the situations and experiences that you go through, will help you to understand later on in your life as such, this recent moment for myself. It's not that I didn't care I always do and want to help the to best of my ability and the information I receive.

But when I did ask the host she said; that the woman stated that I wasn't any good because I didn't pick up on or even mention about her husband, his name or, how he died? Expectation can always bring a moment of clarity to a halt for the rest of the reading as I write, I actually remember the reading went well over the time limit, and I also as a rule tell people they are more than welcome to ask questions during the reading. Now I want to point something out here and that I am in no way defending myself or the outcome of the reading. I am using this as an example for your understandings.

As is usual, often before I head out to do a reading or when clients are coming to the house, I will often get a psychic impression, feeling nausea, or an unsettling feeling, or pain in my back from an injury. This is usually the way and how I choose who goes first for the reading in order to remove the state I'm in. In this case it was a pain in the back area and when asked the client denied having pain, or feeling discomfort?

She then repeated that she was OK and that nothing was wrong, which I was glad to hear but I am now trying to figure out why this is here and what to do with it. So I pressed on with the reading. While this was being done I also remember the client saying no to almost everything and also becoming quite confused herself and a bit irritated. Well the reading ended and she stated she had no further questions, thanked me and went upstairs to join those waiting their turn.

My daughter and wife who attended the party, friends of our meditation hosted the party, and they told me when they heard that that woman was quiet the rest of the time, also that it was confirmed that she fell earlier that week and hurt her back. I didn't tell her about the husband because I figured since she was there she already knew what happened. IN any case, the host stated that she admitted to trying to test me, and I apparently failed. Oh well, if that was what she was expecting from the reading then obviously she got what she came for. Do I feel guilty or should you if you ever experience this? I will simply answer, No. Don't mind me I just hate having my time wasted when someone else could have been there in her place and besides I hate being lied to no matter how spiritual I am or those whom I work with.

You see even after all these years you will still run into this sort of thing and they will also yell at you during readings and swear at you as they leave, trying to make you feel guilty, test you, annoy you but remember I asked if you really wanted to do this, then if so, your going to need really thick skin or a good backbone! I actually have 6 more readings booked for tonight at the same place in Niagara Falls, Ontario Canada. Thanks to people like Wenda, and also to all the other people/clients and friends over the years who have sought me out for guidance through this work, without you, this could never have been. I know the title deserves some insight and that just what I am beginning to do, sorry about the monkey mind. (a term I use whenever my thoughts wonder off)

During your stages or experiences with this psychic advantage in the point of your life you will sometimes come into the different levels of the spirit world, the vale as it is also referred to. In the context of your development, you may find that you begin to make out the feeling or presence and even the visualization and interaction with ghost or spirits? As you become more adapt, you will ultimately attract those to you who know and understand that you can help bring some connection or communication to a family member, loved one or friend.

You may even be able to help them cross over into the spirit world. Truly anyone can do this, but as we have it fear is taught, and it is fear that prevents you from believing in yourself. Often times seeking mine or another persons help who is experienced in what some may call spirit rescue, or house cleaning, not that kind though I am a neat freak and love to clean the house and move my furniture around every 3-5 months. Maybe that's how poltergeist start . . . lol actually its not funny, but what the heck got to laugh and smile at some things right? When you become more confident and have experience, which is our greatest teacher, you may just want to focus on this and not provide readings for anyone.

This if I haven't already said, it is a spiritual journey and is YOUR journey, not anyone else's. Those who know they can trust you will find you at the weirdest places like Starbucks and over heard via conversation they are looking for help or that they have someone in need of assistance, and are looking for someone, take advantage of the moment and speak up, you may be surprised they were sent to see you in the first place. Remember there are no coincidences and everything happens for a reason! Psychic people are like a phone booth to the spirit world where, both worlds can make toll free long distance call.

A ghost in my definition is someone who for whatever reason is either confused or chooses to not cross over, and a spirit is one who has crossed over or if not yet done so, is in the midst of doing so, until they complete whatever it is they feel they have to do. I have met many spirits who don't really care for being called a ghost. So I try to be specific when it counts, and that's just me.

"It is said that there is a fear amongst talking about what is unseen, out of punishment of the unknown and that the process of any such communication is impossible, impossible until you then try and see that the possibilities were there all along, hidden away from those who find it impossible to accept anything but what their told to believe."

Samuel

CHAPTER 14

Your Local Psychic, Everyone Has One

These folks can be found in every city and town, because they are just like us as we are like them and round and round it goes. If you're not inclined to do readings and this is just an interest point to read then great and thanks all the same. If you are considering visiting a psychic, research one that you find as trustworthy as you can.

Word of mouth is good and not so good, depending on the circumstances involved such as the lady I had just mentioned about, I don't think she will give high recognition to anyone in the future due to her own experience and again thanks to her, unknowing, has helped set a spot for conversation, see it does all work out, and besides I know that she will get the answers she's looking for. She was just expecting one thing and wasn't open for other information. She will eventually understand that she and everyone else doesn't need a psychic to talk to their loved ones, you do it each day, and if you get anything from this book remember the rules of first and second thought.

I would ask at this point if you are going or are deciding to visit a psychic, what is your reason for going in the first place? I know that it is stated to be a form of entertainment, but this isn't your daily horoscope you read in the paper, not to mean anything is wrong by this, it's just that this all is perceived as such stated. I personally believe it's more than a circus show and stating the latter does much injustice to this as well as the work that others and I do. Psychic counseling shouldn't replace the doctrine of a counselor, psychologist or medical practitioner. Though it does have it's place and to do so, is like asking a priest to remove your spleen. It just doesn't happen . . . well, maybe in the movies or on criminal minds it would? I should send the idea of the priest to them; it would make a good sequel . . . lol

If you're going to a psychic, don't go if you're looking for validation and comfort or curiosity. I guess in the same sense one would seek priest help? I also want to be clear on something, I know that I keep pulling reference to the priest (s), which of lately has received a very bad reputation. But, they do have their place and it is a shame to link all of them in a group for the action of a few. When you seek the guidance of a psychic please understand that they, DON' T KNOW EVERYTHING!

I don't know how many times I have heard those psychic remarks that apply to every angle related such as "I thought you knew that or how come you didn't know or can't you read minds? It does get trying and also adds to the long list of entertainment factors earlier mentioned. I also find it odd that religious people will state that only a priest can speak to GOD or denounce any relation and assistance from angels stating that psychic's are supposed to be getting their answer's from that guy who is supposed to be from below. Yet they cross themselves mentioning the "Holy Ghost" or the Spirit of Christ and others alike.

Church is instilled by man who is said to be a spin-off, layman's terms that had preached to the many who would sit and listen. Now we have a building, didn't Christ teach in a field or wherever, whenever he had the chance and was done mostly outside? On that note I don't ever think he passed that empty plate to be filled by money or with some churches they demand at least half if not more to what you earn. I will also tell you that the Roman Diocese is a mufti—billion rich society and still passes this plate, and let's not get off topic. If and when you do decide whether or not to go to a psychic, I will say that it should be done with a bit of caution.

Remember, due to others who are only seeking their agenda there are those who you would refer to as a fake, though as I said before, we are all psychic, true but you may meet some who are not seeking to help you the way you think, and is why I am cautioning you. The other fact is simply because; your placing yourself in front of a stranger to step into your personal business not to mention is charging you for the services and time.

You want someone who is confident in themselves and will make you feel comfortable, just for starters. If your going to see someone regarding a loved one or friend who has just passed, then the human side in me will caution you to wait a period of time to and allow the grieving process to take place and after about 6 months to a year, when your head is a bit more clear; you may find you have a better experience from the reader. Otherwise, you may fall onto each and every word that is said and may not get the reading your expecting resulting in a bad experience. I personally do not think that anyone can CALL a family member to you by demanding them to show on command and anyone who tells you they can, may just be full of it.

After finishing the readings for night, I have had people say that they were hoping for so n so to come with any type of message and I explain why they may not be there because I can't nor would I demand any spirit to show unless seriously warranted and there is a time and place for that

Other reasons for a loved one not to show in a reading is because of many variables, you feel sick and you are not picking up anything, the client is afraid, or that (spirit) person may be busy? Yes, they do things on the other side much to what they always wanted to but either; they didn't get a chance or may be something that they always wanted to experience in the physical life and for whatever reason could not? Going to any psychic should be a good experience; I personally don't focus on the negativity of a reading as, this is way to easy and as humans were too sustainable to the outcome even at our own subconscious.

Research the Internet, but I would think that word of mouth would serve just as well because, there may be [psychics in your local area that people may not have a clue about and may even live right beside you? Understand that psychics are not alike each has a different style of psychic development, some may connect right away with you and others may not. In the end, excuse the pun; you will know when to go and who to see. I wish you the best of experiences, validation and, clarity in your search.

"To seek of your own, is to search for that answer there inside of your essence, Spirit or soul. It is here which lies all the answers to the universe that you seek. Often times out of fear, many are afraid to look deep within by quieting their monkey mind or racing thoughts and, listen quietly to that voice within you, which will tell you what you like to know and, what it is your searching for. There lies your true psychic."

Samuel

CHAPTER 15

A World Of Ridicule

Most of the times when you hear people talk about the paranormal or psychic's, there is a mixture of comments to those who love the idea, topic or have been to or want to visit somewhere haunted or a psychic just for the experience, which isn't bad. It is the thoughts and thinking of those who would rather tell them their more than a little nuts to even consider the idea and then brief them on their religious personal adaptation and viewpoint of why not to believe or thinking to even get involved is a bad idea let alone get involved in such nonsense. I say rightfully so for those who choose not to believe in any of this and as I always tell people who try to convince me otherwise, wait until you get to heaven, then we will see I was right . . . lol

Anyhow, these people who choose not to believe is their right but I just wish they would keep their comments and feelings to themselves, rather than trying to promote their idea of righteousness. It all gets repetitive if you know what I mean, besides, like myself and those who chose to become awakened for a reason, in order to help others in spirit and in the physical world of existence out our own free will and desire.

You would think that in our day and age of development, we would not be afraid of the unknown yet here we are ready to rumble on those from another planet who dare to invade. To that idea, there already here and have been for a long time. Really, do you think we are the only things that exist in our solar system or others far greater in size? It is said that a world that doesn't understand what it cannot explain lives in fear.

Now, I'm not saying this to cause trouble, this is much different than what's on the surface. What I am referring to is what society often deems as abnormal is really normal, to go against what were meant to do or our human nature is what is abnormal. When you decide to venture into this interest or lifestyle, I would caution you on who you wish to tell this to, because there are those for whatever reason and, as always, religion has a big part in this due to it's instilled and brainwashed idea that what your doing is either evil or the devils work, quoted from experience speaking to those with the religious background and faith. Faith as I said before is great and I don't want to seem as if I am constantly knocking it, it's the political avenue to which I am always referring to based on its actions to teach through fear in order to gain their trust.

You will also find ridicule in the context of someone blaming you for a reading not going their way or what you have told them didn't come to fruition as fast as they would like. Once there was a lady who attended our meditation class I teach and during the evening I decided to allow Samuel and Sacreah to speak to the people there that night, this is also called channeling.

During this reading, I had a lady ask a question of my guides, I guess from what I can make out they had spoken to her about a move, which she stated wasn't happening, then they told her she was moving to Buffalo. I guess she laughed off the idea and, stated she's never moving to the USA let alone Buffalo NY. About a year or so later I received a e-mail from her and it was something like this . . . Hi Gordon, I am not sure you remember me or not? I was so n so, and the one who was angry with your guides for telling me I am going to move to Buffalo. She hated the city and even mentioning it made her furious.

She continued to say in the email that; she actually did move to Buffalo, not Buffalo NY, USA but a small township called Buffalo. It's a wonderful place and my life is doing well, and does continue from there. Nice validation and also lets you know that messages from spirit don't always mean what we think it does.

I wanted to give you a brief synopsis of what you may expect as I said each is to there own and are different from each other, well in the physical. Some of the things you hear will be cruel and hurtful especially where it comes from a good friend, family member, siblings or even your parents, which my mother (grandmother) absolutely hated the thought of such a thing and ordered me never to speak of it. Especially to her new husband, a devoted faith person, nice guys all the same. Trust me, if you are willing to grow thick skin and you will also gather around you those searching you out for help not to mention you will always have company of your guides and angels. I figured it would be nice to let you know that this is a bit of something that you may and can expect and the fact that if you understand that none of this is your fault, and then you will adjust just fine and overcome it as I did.

CHAPTER 16

The Aftermath of Your Family

In this part of the book I wanted to touch on this subject because it is our hardest teacher given the fact that, they are mostly who we depend on for guidance and support. Not all family members especially parents now a days would admit that they have a son or daughter that is a practicing psychic. Mainly for the basic reason that there lies a fear of ridicule and a discourse of comments best to be avoided. As previously mentioned earlier on in the book depending on the type of upbringing you are birthed into, you may or may not stand on good grounds to enlist such a claim to any of the family especially your parents or grandparents.

To those who are lucky enough have been either raised in a family that is accepting of the "new age ways" you are able to practice your gifts without being ridiculed. You, who are the, lucky individuals, have values that are very open minded and honest, because of the influence of those parents or grand parents who nurture the experience and existence of such wonderful things. To the other side of the cooing there is the family that from either traditional or religious values will smite the thought into oblivion. Especially given their beliefs and where they have come from which is often a place of religious installations and fears of the unknown or that which is not understood.

I was excited to share an experience with my grandmother, who adopted me and raised me as her son, about a television station offering me a chance to apply for a job dealing with the paranormal and my psychic ability. When I called her, and began to explain to her about the opportunity I had she had these beautiful words of expression . . . I don't want you to come her and stop bringing that (swearing) crap and idea you have, I don't believe in it or you and think your full of . . . well you get the idea. A woman who when her late husband passed years ago was telling me about seeing him come through this light in the bedroom, and was reading one of Sylvia Browns books I had lent her.

Wow, needless to say I didn't go, besides being really hurt again is the usual thing with her, but you can't blame a kid for trying to impress his mother. Now I would like to point out that this isn't the case for everyone, because of a better understanding of psychic ability, society has come more accepting of this and is not something that is kept in the dark away from other people's earshot. Point of interest, read "J.Z. Knight's" first book you 'll see what I mean, (She channels a Spirit named Ramtha) and given the time-period which it was wrote, it's a good example. Or go to the older bookstores where I got mine and I also bought it for a great price! Sorry J.Z . . . But I enjoyed it nonetheless.

Depending on your family and upbringing and understanding or religion they may or may not accept the idea of having a psychic in their family and I will be the first ones to tell you like it is and, like mine, even disown you for it, even my older daughters don't believe in me, although it's funny because each of them are awakened but due to their relations they have a fear of staying the opposite. Too bad they were a lot smarter on their own. Regardless how I or they feel their children will do the same thing to them when the time comes and one day realize becoming awakened is not so bad?

So, I said I wanted to speak on the aftermath of family, which I did and hope you learn to have that thick skin not thick head, that comes from EGO, which my girls have learned from their mother. With this understood the aftermath will have no bearing on your need or desire to learn, experience and move forward to a better understanding of where we all come from and where we are all going in the end of our time as humans.

"In time, there will be a place where your family will come to understand that what they have chosen to forget in the physical life, will become awakened to the fullest of understandings about this psychic existence not just with you but, among themselves when they all come home/heaven. Try to understand that the experience you have with them in this life is set in motion to help assist you in learning how to adapt to those moments or experiences in order to develop you own understandings of your life. All is happening for a reason, set in motion by the Universe."

Solis

CHAPTER 17

Influence and Spiritual Messages

Here we will discuss the senses that you will come to learn to attune to if you haven't already. I am sure that most of this, if not all, should relate to you through experience or out of pure interest. Samuel has mentioned that there will be more psychic development course/classes, which are becoming more prominent now days. Such as was in the times of our known King Arthur regarding, "Merlin the Magician".

It wasn't all about science though, it played a big factor, not to mention that he was also an adviser in many areas to the king and; the study of spirituality was also evolved with the kings upbringing well into his years of life. We have all sorts of validated accounts brought though influence of others that often times reach a mass of people to either wake them up by planting a small seed and this is done through movies. These instances of ideas are placement into the mind of its creators, story lines that are influenced by Spirit.

Such movies you may have already seen and if not, well we will state that they are worth viewing if nothing you get out of it, it will be none the less entertainment. Such movies are "What dreams may come" with Robin Williams, "City of Angels" with Meg Ryan and, Nicholas Cage and Nicole Kidman in "The others" which was one of my favorites and one with Matt Damien called, "Hereafter". All are pretty much in line with what it is like to be psychic or angels or dealing with the spirit world or the paranormal. Remember, that each experience is different or similar depending on you and that other individual. These give some sort of idea of what is like on the other side.

Through use of your senses of your visualization, you will come to learn that through meditation it will often give your best and in some cases, the most experience with your guides or angels. This is basically related to your sixth sense and how you may go about to use it to connect with your guides or angels. Now, I want to tell you right off the bat that I don't have the perfect formula or answer as to what will work best for you in this section.

Only because, you are unique and special for your own process of learning through your personal development and understandings. It's not that I can't tell you, on the contrary, I will try as best that I can but, it is ultimately up to you and what your willing to practice. I would also like to note that if you already know how to do all of this which is stated in my book then, close your eyes, take a deep breathe/exhale and let go of all that you claim to know to allow more room or other ideas that may actually benefit yourselves.

I am always willing to try new ideas on how to do things different and to think that I know everything would only allow for the EGO to grow and not myself. Practice, the art of allowing, not trying to do anything. What I mean by this is try not to force the result of your development or mediation; the frustration is constant and only builds more and more. By meditating your also learning to develop the art of allowing. This not only allows you to relax it allows for your vibration to move at a much higher rate towards that of the Spirit World

When you do meditate try to be consistent, meaning the same time every-time. This allows you to prepare yourself and, your surroundings, also to get into the zone. While in this meditative state, through practice these visualizations will become clearer and descriptive. You may even hear your voice aloud verbally through this session? I know that once your thoughts become calmer, you may seem as if your falling asleep and find yourself traveling somewhere and meeting individuals or even animals.

The messages if you remember from the beginning of the book learn to allow for the rule of first thought, by where guides and angels will communicate? As I said each person is different and so are the experiences they receive during the meditation seating. I have while meditating met my angels and guides and know that this could also work for you. I will speak a bit more on meditation in the next chapter.

Try not to forget about the rule of second thought versus the first thought whenever you are meditating. Your visualizations are important and you should always be documenting your own experiences. As we move into this area of our discussion meditating practice is a very big help and will help with your psychic development. Now understand, that this practice is about being in the present moment, a lot of this relates to Buddhist and Zen practice that has transformed and evolved over thousands of years from Buddha and has proven to be most effective in every area of your life and your body. Literally everything is affected when you begin to meditate, not to mention that it is a proven stress reliever. As I have mentioned, that this practice and so called it that because you will eventually move from practice to an everyday part of your daily things you do. It is a lifetime practices that only gets better and better. When we practice meditating, we learn to allow thoughts to be present and also to tune away, not out other sounds.

A few funny things can also happen when meditating, while you are quiet, Children and animals seem to want to constantly be around you. That's if you have them and this is due to the energy that is caused by you meditating. It's a universal release and action that takes place in all things and when this energy is closely moving it has an attraction, besides the natural effect that your kids strive for constant attention all the time, especially when your trying to find moments for yourself.

Meditating is about not just relaxation, although it plays a big part, but learning to become aware of yourself and your thoughts. It is through the practice that when you have done it enough regularly, you will begin to develop visions or visualizations of places, past, present, and future though they all exist simultaneously. It is here also, that your guides and angels will begin to communicate with you. I can't tell you at this precise moment what you will see or experience because . . . . are you not paying attention, to your individuality. In addition, your probably wondering how to meditate or even begins and, there are a few ideas that I can give you.

First, you can attend a meditation circle in your community, usually word of mouth or on the Internet is a good source to search. This allows you to make a choice and to search a place that suites your need and comfort level which is very important for the obvious reason.

On this note I would also like for you to be aware of some of these places because some are EGO induced, or have a strict regiment about meditation geared out of their own agenda. A Buddhist temple is a good place to start and they are always more than accommodating to you in helping you in this quest.

Through your daily practice of meditation, you will soon learn that these mentioned senses will literally come alive in you. As an example, I will give you one of my own experiences. I used to work at the Seneca Casino in Niagara Falls N.Y as a Gaming inspector. One night I was in the back room where they count all the money, there are usually bins that held the different currency of coin and they were in the different colors of red, blue, yellow and green.

Now, it was about that time . . . halfway when everything got quiet. For some reason I looked over at these bins and was strangely surprised that they were all brand new bins? I was told that the boxes were not even changed and questioned if I was either really tired or hallucinating? I was so amazed all those colors seemed to have a perfect glow of each individual color that was so intense! As that portion of the shift ended and as I continued my constant day of walking for 8 hrs., I saw every machine in that place and, each color was new, everything had a clean glow of distinct energy of perfect color with everything. This was just an example of one of the many things I have experienced from meditating.

Now your psychic impressions, I think may be much different than the actual visualization. Impressions are fed through your thought where the information is coming from spirit and those from the spirit world. This doesn't mean that you can go out and rob the store then blame it on your spirit guides. That is second thought, your thought and often that of a lower vibration.

It can also be said that they can sometimes influence through the emotional state of drug induced habituates and alcohol. Due to the levels of vibrations, they literally feed on you and your energy, which can make you both physically sick and depressed. But not to worry your state of mind should at this point focus on the positive especially through this stage of your learning.

Only because at the beginning stage of anything you should always try to allow those more experience to deal with those thought formed elements. Enough of that for now as we will save it for discussion at another time. During your stages of meditation and I call it this because of the several learning stages that you need and will learn to deal with, accept and not give it much attention. Allowing your meditations to be a lot more visual and enlightening.

Visualization experience is attainable but may be the way your looking to receive it. You see, not everyone who is psychic gets the same visualizations and feelings, for this part even though we are all one, connected by this, by our choice; to experience the separateness of our spiritual individuality through this process. Other encounters can come from the paranormal events such as experiencing ghost/ apparition or residual energy. Then, there is the other you know is spirit. I want to point something out to you and that is ghost and, spirit are two separate things.

One (spirit) has the ability because, they have completed the process of spiritual rebirth into the spirit world and can make visitations a lot more clearly than that of ghost who either, are stuck for some reason that is keeping them here. Some are stuck out of fear, confusion or uncertainty. The other that I have mentioned is residual energy, which basically means the action is an imprint in time that plays over and over such as a video recording. Such as the girl, who is seen in the garden walking at 10pm repeatedly, just as an example.

Often people or yourself have already had some kind of paranormal experience or, some instance where you may have seen a glimpse of someone, who instantly disappeared just as fast as you thought you had seen them? This isn't a rare occurrence, though some may be attributed to a psychological memory imprint of an event that has already taken place where, your mind records and it automatically plays back not in its entirety but enough to grasp what your mind will allow at that precise moment?

Hey I had to give those who choose not no believe in all of this mumbo jumbo, a shot . . . lol. I had often thought that if it couldn't be broken down, dissected, or cured, that it may never be accepted by the base population of general society or of those in power positions. But there is a greater understanding and study that is being performed to really credit or discredit the whole subject of the paranormal, which is both good and, not so good. The natural fact remains that to throw away something that may have basis, psychics will have a harder time with science moving into this world, in order to find any explanation for the paranormal or unexplainable.

This will always be the case as it's implanted into our thinking of second thought via religion or family values that, it is much too easy to just accept it or believe.

CHAPTER 18

Meditation

As I have briefly mentioned, meditation is an important part towards developing your psychic abilities. It will help you more, than you realize. When deciding to practice, I suggest from all the number of years not only teaching meditation but also applying it myself; I usually set up some area that is comfortable and, quiet. I also would like to remind you to remember that you are only human and that life will get in the way where you may not have the time to meditate or practice at the same time, which in itself can be frustrating.

The point of meditating is to relax, so when you can, meditate. Don't worry about it. Just do it whenever you get the chance, no worries. Let's start with explaining how to go about how to meditation. Unless you already do this, just hear me out. Find a place either inside or out that is as quiet as can be, for you. Use a small bell or gong, to clear the air before you start to meditate. I use Buddhist symbols, which are good to use. I also light a bees wax candle to help cleans the air or sometimes I will also light some incense such as Nag Champa, which has a pleasant smell.

Once you have that in place, you may start to meditate. Depending on where you are you may want to sit up, as laying down, may lead you into just falling asleep which often can happen when first starting this practice. For sitting you can purchase a meditation chair, or pick up a yoga block at your local sports store. Once you decide to meditation find the time that best suits you. I usually do this after I got home to help me to unwind or during the day where my employers set aside a prayer room that I can meditate and others to pray given their religion. Being consistent with the time help greatly as well as gave me something to look forward to.

Now, you may want to try meditation for a 15-minute duration. Gradually, you can add more time depending on your monkey mind. When this happens just allow whatever thoughts come in to do so recognize them and breathe, eventually this will help you to relax your thoughts aka monkey mind. There is no right or wrong way to practice, but I will tell you that there are several ways to meditate.

Another thing I do with our meditation class is walking meditation, remaining silent and absorbing the understanding of all elements around you by walking; you take notice in everything you do with each step.

That's a little too much at this part so lets just stick to the seated meditation. Your chair should be somewhat comfortable and I will tell you to be mindful of your legs if you cross them as, they may just fall asleep if you don't.

If you do fall asleep don't worry about it, it does happen and I often tell people if they do at our meditation, it's a compliment to our home and us because they must feel comfortable. If this continues to happen, try not to attempt this when you're sleepy, sick or feeling ill, and under any habituates. Besides the fact that you'll ruin the whole experience and may see something you may not want; remember that thought creates action.

Also, you may want to keep a small book to write down your experiences. This will also help you to validate your experience, which will help with the psychic awakening for you? You can also go to the Buddhist temple or check your local colleges and universities who, may hold interest courses. Also, you can do this with a group of friends, place the chairs in a circle or you may even choose to sit on the couch, either is OK and makes no difference. If anything . . . you will come out more calm and relaxed sometimes often better than a full night sleep.

Meditation is about you and, no one else.

There are several books written on the subject, but I suggest you check the Internet, or my own website: **"theguidancewithin.com"**

CHAPTER 19

Practice, Practice and More Practice!

These words ring in my thoughts more times than I would like to admit, I also remember the rule of being human as Samuel reminds me, then I find the time to meditate and, all is a lot better. This is very important as I may have said about a lot of things in this book but it couldn't be further than the truth. Not meant to be a pain or something you regret doing and, is also another reason why I had asked if you're serious about doing this, developing your psychic ability earlier on in the book. As you pick up on this and become more awakened, yes more via practice, dealing with every situation, person and, cultural differences and, beliefs.

By practicing will help you to learn how to deal with a lot of different or same situations and how to handle them. It also will help you to build on your confidence and, trust of yourself, guides and angels. Even today I practice what I preach and when I forget my wife and best friend Lezlie, who is always there for me as are my guides and angels, reminds me. I thank them each and all . . . Samuel, Sacreah, Sebastian, Solis, Youngam, Joanna, Rista, Chin who has been with me in this life and has also been with me in all my past lives. It is something I continuously look forward to.

Here is a final message from Samuel, Sacreah until, the next time:

Understand at those moments in your life when all seem lost or unbearable, you may call us to arms to assist you in whatever you need. Be specific to our assigned duties, in order to help in our tasks, and we ask of you; to trust in us, within your hearts if not with your own eyes. With Angels wings we bless and keep you forever in time.

CHAPTER 20

Letting Go and Going Home

Finally, we end here. Well, not really ends accept the fact that we have reached the end of this first book. I wanted to touch a little on this fact of knowing what you do as opposed to those individuals who may not, such as, your grandparents, elders, those who may have for whatever reason a fear, about what comes after this life? Someone once asked me how do you know that there truly is something after this life?

I can say that my response was pretty quick only because I have personally experienced it more than once. The first time, I don't remember how it happened, but I remember the experience of drowning when I was about 3 or 4 years old and I had woken up in a hospital,. (By the way I what know what you may be thinking but, I have a great memory especially when it comes to something such as this).

I was in a hospital bed that had plastic all around me; it felt as if I were in a triangular bubble with a wide type zipper, on my left side. As I was sitting up on the bed I looked around and saw blue small bathtubs in the middle of a large room. The sun was shining in from window lighting up the room with sunbeams on the floor. I also noticed kids, all sort of kids, in this room in beds just like mine and some running around and playing, others having a bath in the small tubs. Then I saw older people, I am speaking about the nuns. They wore the old style habits, which were dark blue with suspender type garment on their chest with a white apron. I noticed that their hats in particular were very funny looking. They looked like moons on their heads some nuns wore the black outfits and others seem to be nuns but wore worker type clothing. As I stared at what was happening I heard a sound to my left which was the zipper being undone and a pretty lady in the blue work clothes said, OK Gordon now its your turn, she then took me and undressed me and I had my turn in the bath. Funny I don't remember the water but I knew I was in there as I smiled and laughed with the other kids.

Time ended and I was placed back into my bed with fresh sheets and a warm blanket. As the lady was zipping up my plastic see through tent, she said there you go well as new, go to sleep now. I also remember from that time on I was visited by a man with a hat who would come every time it was my birthday and stated to me that I will die when I am 26 years old, over the years this became normal to me until the year of my 26th birthday.

This leads into the second experience . . . As I told you I had a recurrence of a spirit visitor of this guy who, would show up out of the blue and, remind me that on my 26th birthday I will have a end to my life. Well to try to keep the story short, I have tried to tell people, basically some family members with them replying I was full of it or to go away, grandmothers words again.

Then the day of my 26th birthday came and I didn't even notice that the guy didn't show up? I was at my older sister Cathy's house, one summer night. No this isn't going to be a romance novel. I was at her home one evening and was planning on working on my car to repair an idler arm; this is not only under the car but helps to control the steering. I pulled the car inside while my sister and friends were in the home having a party. I jacked up the car and made all the preparations to safely secure it with not just one jack but two on the front supported with some old tires under the sides, you know just in case . . . lol I then placed an old red clean rag under the spot where I would be working and where my head would rest out of the dirt.

As I went under the car and began to loosen the nut or what it was I would do to fix this, I heard my name called. I stopped yelled back and no one answered thinking I was hearing something? Again I resumed my repair when I heard it again accept from a different spot in the garage, I stopped looked around to see if someone was goofing off but no one was there.

This happened a few more times and the last time a voice said get out from under the car. All of a sudden, I suddenly felt a jolt in my body, and felt as if someone grabbed my legs, then the next thing I remember I was sitting on an air plane looking out the window of the plane. I had no idea what or where I was going? Then I remember looking at the clouds and then this male flight attendant wheeled his cart from the front and said; well Gordon, have you made up your mind yet?

I looked at him without a though and said, I'm going to stay. What seem to be seconds, I felt a rush overwhelm me as if I just dropped off the peak of a very high roller coaster. I found myself getting up from the concrete floor of the garage where I was originally laying. Someone who I felt that had hold of both my legs pulled me out from under the car and, as soon as I rolled to get on my feet, the car slammed down on top of that cloth exactly where my head would have been! Talk about almost wetting yourself. I immediately looked around and found no one in the garage accept for myself and the chills that were running all over my body. I also avoided that place for almost three weeks after telling my sister what has happened. I later found out that it was my baby brother "Roger", who I never met, pulled me out; he died at an early age of crib death.

So with these lasting examples, I just wanted to give you an answer to the question you will no doubtfully hear if not have yourself and, that is . . . is somewhere we go when we leave here? I would and, always answer yes from personal experience. And, I know for a fact that there is much more than the world we live in. The world is a much larger picture of our existence than we could ever imagine!! It's like I said in the beginning, I'm not here to convince you or anyone else, I know what I know.

What and how I know, through the teachings of Samuel and, Sacreah and by other Spirit Guides and Angels; which I chose to share with you. "This gift" if you like to refer to it, is within each of us all. It takes only a fraction of your intention to see it.

I wish through the grace of mother father god and everything in the universe that, you experience in this life and wish you the best on this adventure as you, become awakened.

In Love and Light,

Samuel & Sacreah and yours truly . . .

To Be Continued . . . .

OLE-object

Words from Website

A thought to share with all of you a question that is most often asked of me regarding your spirit guides?

I am often asked, why can't I see them but you can?

This attempt is sometimes difficult to communicate at first and often takes a lot of energy and there are other spirits who may find it easier? Like all humans not all spirits are the same.

Other reason's may be that they don't want to frighten you. This is just one example as to why you may not be able to see them. Another reason is that you may not truly want to see anything; out of fear, which is often taught by society.

For this reason, they will appear in your dreams or use some other way to try to communicate, through your "rule of first thought."

Other times, you may want to see them so very much, your hard efforts will create a block. Which won't allow your sensitivity to feel their presence or hear their voice?

Through your own preseverence, you can develop and communicate and contact your guides/angels as well as, your family members, and even pets.

To do this… try this as a simple guideline to follow. You will need to learn to develop your patience and allow for time to meditate. Knowing that those who have crossed over or passed from the physical essence are never far away from our thoughts.

Know that I have faith in you. Stop trying so hard. They are always with you and in your heart. I understand as human beings we have the need to hug and hold them forever. So, say what you can to those you love at this moment, tell them how much you care and love them.

While in the physical world, remember that it's never too late to restart your relationship. Saying you're sorry doesn't mean your wrong or week. It just means you have enough love, strength and courage within you, to create change in your life.

By doing this, you will avoid any regret of not saying how you feel. Take the time to share any favorite memories you have and at this moment thank them for who they are because, when there no longer here; you may just regret the time that has passed.

...From Samuel and Sacreah

Words from Website

Help Me Understand;

What It Is, That You Don't Want To Hear?

Many people have come to me for readings through the years seeking answers, clarification and a sense of reunion or connection with those whom have passed over. There are other reasons they may choose to see me for a reading, but lets stick to the example that I had just mentioned. Before I begin to do any reading(s), I often introduce the angels and guides that I work with. I feel that it is always a good start to help the clients become comfortable and relaxed as they can. When some people visit a psychic for the for time they are very nervous and are afraid they are going to hear something bad. I assure you, this is more common than you can ever imagine. I still get nervous from time to time doing readings or lectures. It happens and there is nothing to worry about, as Samuel always used to tell me; remember you're human first and foremost.

I have mentioned in this book that, "everyone" is psychic. Each of us may have different psychic abilities and always can be tuned through practice and meditation. It may not always apply to everyone; some are born more tuned to their psychic ability and with the proper guidance will become well known psychics. I also would like to expose a psychic taboo or secret, not every psychic knows everything! As far as I know neither I, nor any other psychic I know, holds any superpowers that I'm aware of? As psychics, many of us, like you, will make mistakes. It's bound to happen and is always part of the makeup of the universe that assists us by always tuning our abilities from our experience(s).

Many people seeking psychic guidance are often not sure what it is that there looking for? Some people may come to you to solve their worldly issues and are not always ready to hear what is said. Not that you should even solve their issues, remember your assisting in their guidance and not to influence their decision. That's for them to do. I have a question for you, when you decide to visit a psychic, what is it that your looking to get out of the reading?

Many people you will also soon learn that people coming to a reading or psychic party don't believe in this psychic stuff. Often looking for proof, some as I said may be unsure of what to expect and others may be looking for a "WOW" factor. In those instances people are often disappointed with the result. What they hear is not always what they want.

I ask myself, whose fault is this? The psychic or yours? In some cases, it may be both. When someone visits me for a reading, they may, not even listen to the information that is coming through expecting only to hear from a certain family member by exact name rank and serial number. When they may hear from another family member who has information for them, they will often tune this information out and state at the end they didn't hear what they expected or get a visit from a certain person, therefore the reading wasn't any good. Whenever this happens, which is not very often, I say the blame is entirely theirs. Just because they didn't hear what they wanted or from whom they wanted, doesn't mean you are a bad psychic you can only tell then what you are getting, because if you start telling them what they want you are not being true to yourself or your guides.

As a client and the reader, your attitude is everything. Psychics may only get so much information at one time; some may be able to read for you where others may not? I say, if you are not willing be open with that information, and then you come as a closed book. The information from Spirit comes to you for your best interest they see, and doesn't often come with the winning Lottery numbers, or I wouldn't be here...lol

Not everything you hear will be exactly what you expect. Remember, your clients are the one's who allow the information to flow or not, it's all about the attitude.

Words from Website

Angels and guides are often misunderstood and snubbed at the idea of their existence; from our own doubts or that, which has been taught through influences such as; society, education, families, religions or other experiences in our lives. Angels are always there, constantly working among you and I. Often times, without us even noticing; we are most often too involved with other things in our lives that we often miss their messages, or signs of their presence. My guides, Samuel and Sacreah are exactly that... angels. I refer to them for other people's sake as; my spirit guides. This way many folks accept it easier.

I teach people at my psychic development classes to pay attention to the rule of first thought, as you have come to learn about in this book. Whenever they appear I have people express the overwhelming presence of love, I like to refer to as "happy tears" but this isn't the only way. I have been introduced through meditations to other angels and guides and to others who are not angels but known as a group called "the watchers." The angels are directed in their duties from our mother/ father god to serve through the greatest good of their own as well as, our individual developments in life. Whenever you need help, ask for those angels or guides for assistance, but be particular what you would like help with. Just as your asking for help from a friend here in the physical world. Angels cannot interfere without your permission in your daily life of experience without your permission that is a universal law.

Many of the angels have names but the intent of asking is key and the name is for our own sake of attachment. They know your intent, and like us, are bound by guidelines of the universe. You can ask assistance from angels of mercy or archangels such as Michael, Uriel, or Sebastian. You more than welcome to ask for assistance from my angels Samuel or Sacreah. Angel's can assist us in helping with healing wounds both, mentally and physically. Along with courage, and protection.

Angels are assigned to everyone, and no one is without. We humans are stuck to many attachments such as names, but I would like for you to know that by our unintentional thought, or when we ask for their help aloud, or in prayer they are there with us before, we are finished requesting their assistance. Nice arrangement don't you think?

Words from Website

Lastly, I want to thank you for taking the time not only to purchase this book but, by opening your thought and understanding that you, are as psychic as I or any other in this world we live in. Furthermore, understand that just because others in this world may not believe in as you do or, are seeking the same life experiences. This is okay. Do this for yourself. Your path in life can change whenever you like, you can change the direction where your life is heading at any moment. freewill is, and will be forever yours. This is the universal law.

I want to thank Balboa press and it's staff for assisting me with this growth of the book, and the very last, I would especially like to thank my wife, and our daughter "squeak" for editing this book.

In Love and light,
Samuel and Sacreah

REFERENCES

1. Google Home Page

2. Wikipedia

3. The Bible

4. My Guides/Angels

5. Photograph by Wendy Teal,
   website: http://wendyinfocus.500px.com/

   You are invited to visit my web site at:
   www.theguidancewithin.com